Printed in Poland by Amazon Fulfillment.

ISBN: 978-1-671172-35-7

Note from the Author

Hello and many thanks for choosing this book.

There is an old Quaker saying, 'Let your life speak,' which I believe means that our quest, while we are on this earth, is to find out why we were created, what our purpose or gift is and then; to live life to the full, sharing our gift with the world.

You are unique.
You were born to be you,
Not someone reflected in another's eyes
or wearing a borrowed coat.
But your true self,
In your own place
In your own space
Wearing your own face.

-Wendy Bowers 2018

We live in a time when life seems busier than ever and more than 50% of us report feeling stressed most of the time. We are bombarded with noise and images from multiple channels every waking hour. We are programmed to believe that material things will make us happy.

Sadly, we are not taught to discover and build on our innate gifts. Our education system is designed to educate millions of children to achieve a narrow range of academic goals, and within this system of cramming and testing, it is nigh impossible for over-worked teachers to foster rather than quash individual creativity. Most of us therefore, follow well-meaning advice from parents and peers and base life choices on exam results and job titles that 'spell' success. We do not teach our children to listen to their life and we do not stop to listen to ours.

I finally let my life speak to me in March 2016 whilst recovering from serious ill health, after working myself into the ground for the third time. What followed is chronicled in this book.

I hope you find my story interesting and enjoy the poetry and the walks. But mostly, I hope that this book encourages you to slow down a little and create some space, and in that space, you will hear your own life speak.

Wendy Rowe

December 2019

About the Author

Wendy Bowers is a writer, performance poet and business coach. Her career has taken her from an old disused mill in East Lancashire, where she built a successful manufacturing business with her first husband, to the corridors of Westminster, where she advised the government re the gender pay gap and the Burt Review. Alongside her demanding career, she raised 4 children and increasingly cared for her Mum who was suffering from dementia. After crashing and burning for the third time three years ago, she radically altered the way she lives and works. She now spends her time encouraging others to share her learning via coaching, retreats and workshops.

Wendy lives in a small Lancashire village on the edge of the moors with her hairy husband and long suffering dog – oh sorry, that should read, her long suffering husband and her hairy dog!

You can find out more about Wendy and read her latest poetry and walks here:

https://www.wendybowers.co.uk

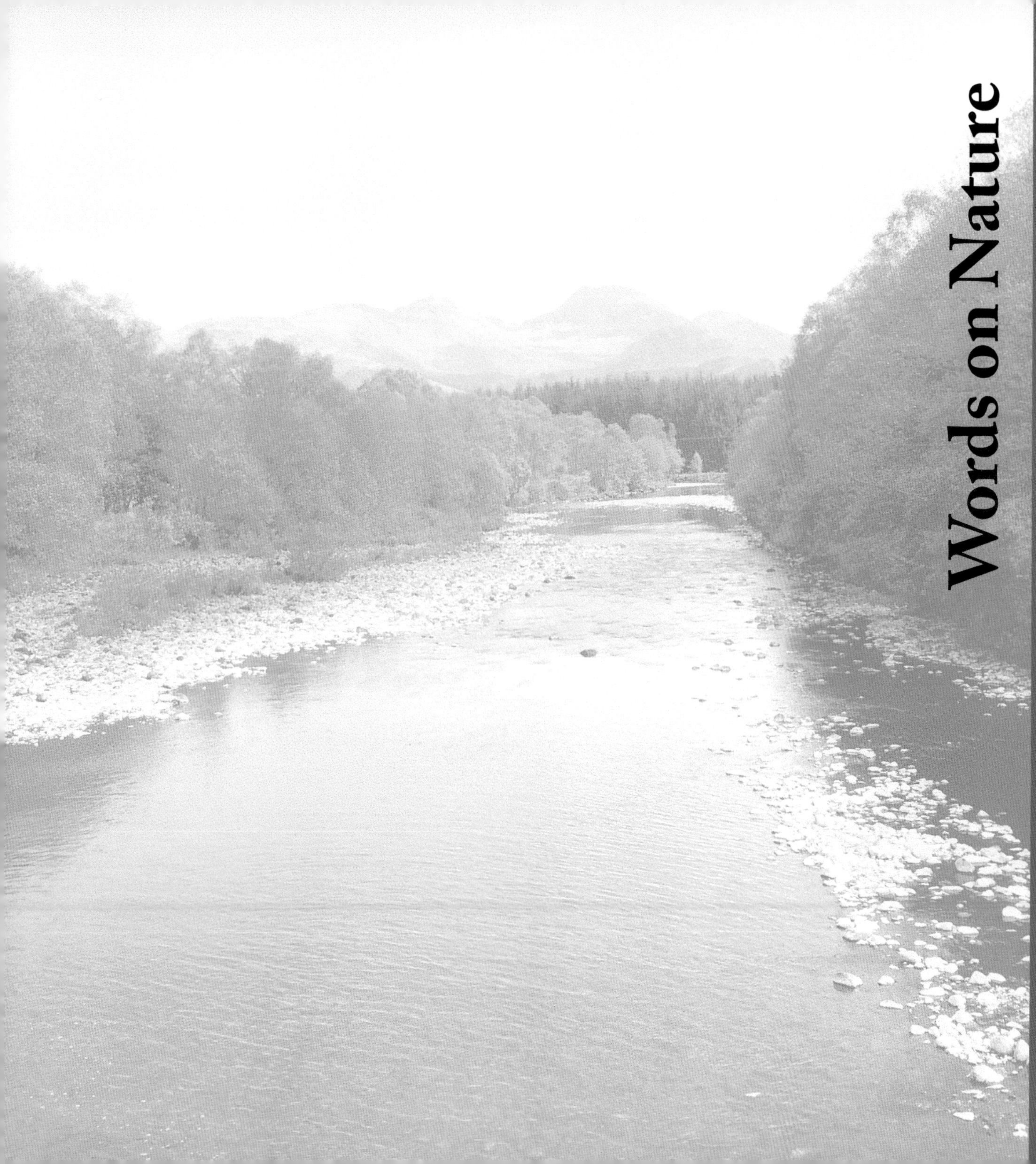

Words on Nature

Waking

The world wakes gently,
Soft light seeping
around the edge of night
as the earth tilts towards the day.

Slowly, shapes come into being
Emerging from the deep dark.
Trees stretch their branches,
Earth and Sky separate.

There is no rush.
The world knows how to wake.
How to welcome every part of its creation
And why the birds sing.

Wake slowly my friend
Slowly like the world
Say your hello sweetly,
As the bird in the tree.

Breathe deeply,
Feel the slow beat within,
Go gentle into each new day
It's not about the win.

Again

And still the moss makes cushions
on the limestone walls
Though the leaves fall and the drizzle
mizzles its way across the moor.
Wet wellies slap my calves
The dog pants and pulls,
Daylight dawdles into dusk
as the cars come home.

These are the days of
green moss and rusted tree,
Full scarlet hips and faded rose
Dark soaked oaks and twisted fern
Drifting smoke as fires burn
Evening walks before we turn
the clocks and cozy down for winter.

Breathe it in, the damp and drizzle all
Soak my skin and let the rain sink in
Smell the crushed and broken leaves
upon the lane
Let me savour
every last whisper of summer
and save it
until it comes again.

Close up

Walking on a sun sharp afternoon
a squally shower surprised me
and I laughing,
ran and found shelter under a tree
by the laneside.
Slow minutes passed as long streaks of wet
soaked the grass and patched the dusty track
with puddles,
Whilst I stayed dry
under the thick canopy
cheating the rain.

Today, on this soft December day
I walked under the trees
unaware that a breeze
was sneaking along sleeping branches,
prodding precocious drops
until, losing their balance,
they tumbled and smashed on my bright blue jacket
and woolly hat.
So it seems my summer shower
Had only been playing hide and seek
And now it splashed my face and shouted
"found you!"
And won the game.

And smiling, with the drops still drying on my face
I strode on into the mist where
the signpost pointed nobody to nowhere
on the moorland track.
I knew the land that surrounded me,
The bulk of Boulsworth to my right
The ridge of Pendle to my left
But nothing and no-one rose out of the grey
To share my day,
So in the quiet I resolved to see the world reflected in a raindrop
And be grateful for the things closest to me
Which can be forgotten when I look at distant views.

Rain Dance

The rain patters on the path
and tyres swish and spray "yesss", "yesss"
where the road dips.

Rain – the first in weeks
and the leaves reach and drench
themselves in cold precipitation,
Flowers drink thirstily
stamens straining to suck the sweetness.

Birds squawk amidst the drumming droplets,
The clouds roll
The windscreen wipers drone
Ladies unfurl umbrellas.

But I stand,
With arms outstretched across the middle of the meadow
and let the rain dance upon my face.

Incredible

On my walk today

I pass:
Old cottages with colour spilling over walls
Blackberries ripening –
Sodden fields where doe-eyed cows
study me as they chew.

I walk:
On a thousand year old track
under a million year old hill.

I step:
On tarmac, pebble, mud and grass
and cross puddles on stones
and streams on wooden bridges.

I see:
Sunlight glinting on green and speckled leaves
and try to catch one as it falls.

I hear:
Water rushing
a tractor idling
birds chirruping.

I taste:
My hot coffee
and later, a cold ice-cream.

My feet are damp, my heart is warm and dry,
I am in awe of these ordinary things
just footsteps from my door
which are in truth, incredible.

Time

Bending low under soft branches I left the path behind
Needing to feel an undiscovered place
like a child first tasting freedom,
crossing the stream, scrambling the bank
without a backward glance to home.

Feeling small amidst a circle of the tallest firs
I watched the trees at play,
branches dancing and swaying,
their tender tips touching,
soothing the restless wind.

Breathing deep the damp of secret spaces
Hearing nothing but the creaking bend
and flexing of the living wood
I sank into the mossy green and let time
enfold me.

My father, you sat with me in the clearing
And saw with me the tiny darting bird
You smelled with me the scent of coming rain
And felt the air begin to cool and change.
And as we rose and found again the path
Leading to the wide and windswept moor
I saw in the fading sun, just one shadow
and heard only my boots on the stony floor.

Grace

Summer seems tired today,
Sun struggling to break through heavy grey,
Even the wind seems slow
as it bends the thistle and rolls soft silken
tufts across the lane.

Time has tangled the hedgerow
where the birds have left their nests,
And bare and broken stalks
divested of their pink and purple dress
shiver in the breeze.

But does the summer rage
against the dying of the light?
Oh what lessons could mere mortals learn.
With quiet grace the season ages,
Shaking loose its leaves
Laying down its fruit
Ready to slip into the sleep of winter
Its job complete.

Boulsworth on a June morning

Boulsworth on a June morning
rain blurring her edges -
Drifting in drizzle to drench the village gardens.

Newly shorn sheep shivering 'neath the slick wet walls
and still the curlew calls
and glides and dips over the heather.

Mist and rain,
Lacing the hedgerows
Frosting the ferns

Washing the waking morning.

Photograph opposite: My son, David, dancing with my mum.

Words on Love & Family

These things that I must do

I do not want to see the things that I am seeing,
I do not want to know the things I have to know,
But down your corridors I dutifully follow
looking at these rooms with their commodes.

Past names and photographs on doors
of Edna, Jean and Bill
whose unknown lives are now distilled
in frames upon on a sill.

And "Bill's brought his piano"
And "Edna likes this chair"
and Jean is talking constantly to someone who's not there.

"How often do you bath them?"
"Are the gardens all secure?"
"Do you have activities? and locks on every door?"

I know the questions to be asked
and what I'm looking for,
My smile is fastened into place
My heart is on the floor.

The Dales, The Crofts, The Summerfields
with their shuffling slippered souls,
Searching the maze of corridors
to find their way back home.

Written after visiting 7 care homes one Saturday to try and find somewhere for my Mum who had mid stage dementia.

On moving my Mum into a home

In the darkness the demons wait
sitting within the shadows of my restless sleep

WAITING, READY, ALERT.

and in that split second of consciousness
they pounce –
and stand in the headlights of my conscience
mocking, daring, glaring, goading me
 to defend, justify, explain my actions once again –

and I am trapped
alone, on a lonely road at night.

No safe retreat to sleep and demons in the road ahead

WAITING, READY, ALERT.

And then they start.

Hurling their accusations
Stoning me with my shame
"Why, why, why" they scream, "are you here with us
again?"
"She's your mother, mother, mother"
"You are selfish, gutless, weak"
"How can you even begin to break,
the promise you said you'd keep?"
"But I am broken, broken, broken"
I scream in silent rage
and the demons gather round to hear
my pitiful tirade –
and they whisper, prod and poke and jab
my heart, my head, my soul
and they snigger in the silent night
and glare with eyes so cold.

And they stay

WAITING, READY, ALERT.

While sleep retreats into a cul de sac
and I am racked with guilt
and dragged into another dawn.

Undone

I am unravelled.

Kinked wool in a skein.

Its all there –
the length of me

But not where –
it's supposed to be.

Could you still knit I wonder
If I placed the needles in your knotted hands?

Is that something you would remember?
A 'knit one, pearl one' revelation.

Are the patterns still there?
The jumper you knitted Dad when you were courting,
Our baby clothes,
Your padded shouldered eighty's two-piece,
Your designs the envy of your friends.

Knit me a memory Mum
One of yours –

Without you knowing the stitches of my life

I am undone.

Scones

I promised you scones
and so I baked them
brought them with jam and cream,
warm and fragrant –
Knowing that you would not remember
I had promised.

I promised you scones
and so I placed one in your hand
spread with jam and cream
warm and fragrant –
Knowing that you would not remember
What you'd eaten.

I promised you scones
and so I gently wiped your mouth
smeared with jam and cream,
and held your hand
Knowing that you would not remember
Who I was.

I promised you scones.

The Book

Through the long weekend
of my daughter's labouring
and my mother's leaving
I read you

When the conflict of hope and wonder
and loss and futility clashed like swords
and cleaved my heart in two
I read you

In the warm sun of the morning
Sipping my tea and
waiting for the news
I read you

In the long, long moments
of the ink dark night
as nurses tip-toed on rubber soles
I read you

As a thousand thoughts swam and
surged and rolled
in the sea of my imaginings
You anchored me

And when the first call came
I dropped you in an instant
Leaving your words pressed on the garden table
As I ran shouting with joy
"She's here"

And when the second call came
You lay forgotten
As I raced past fields and houses
Grappling with the magnitude
of life's leaving.

Later, when my heart stopped
between each laboured breath,
through sleepless hours
I read you

And when the last came
You bore witness
with cover closed
As the story ended.

Life begins and ends
and we are writ upon the pages,
We must read the final lines
and smile and say
"Oh my, that was a good read."
And then turn with anticipation
To the next title.

The book I was reading was 'Spill, Simmer, Falter, Wither' by Sara Baume.
Rosie born 24.2, Mum died 27.2

It's not

It's not in a word
In a line
In a book

It's in a look.

It's not in how far
In how long
In how much

It's in a touch.

It's not in in a ring
In a church
In a place

It's in a space.

It's not in I'm yours
In you're mine
In I've got

It's just not.

Still

When Autumn colours the back of your hands
And there is a stoop to your stand.

You will still be
the one I look up to

and measure all men by.

The wax on the wall

One day, when I am old
Someone will move the piano
Because I have moved on.

"Oh" they will say,
"What's that on the wall?"
and peering close they will
see it's wax, purple wax
dribbled down the wall.

And no-one will be there to recall
why the wax is on the wall.
To tell the story of how we all
for years and years
came together
to share the unfolding of our lives.
Eating together the meals cooked
on busy Saturdays
when the kids were small,
or how we chose our recipes
on tired evenings
in the middle of our lives
and how we told our truths and
lived our fears
and loved for all those years.

No—one will be there to remember
the milestones covered by tablecloths
through the Valentines and Halloweens
and Christmases of our gatherings,
The rush of evening air through the opened door
as friends arrived
making the candles dance
through time.

Someone will scrape the wax off the wall
and paint over the stain,
not knowing how we laughed
as I blew the candle out
tipping the metal holder,
spilling the wax down the back of the piano.
Not knowing how you held me close and said
"no-one will see it, we never move the piano,"
Never knowing that you made me feel like molten wax.

Photograph opposite: My Great Grand-father Albert Strange

Words on Life

Who am I?

I am a million different people
to a million different people

I am a million times me
In a million moments
to a billion different people

Who am I?

I am who you see
I am who you want me to be
I am what I do
I am what I do to you
I am what I feel
I am how I make you feel

I am no-one
I am nothing
I am everything
I am all things
I am here
I am now
I am life
I am love.

Just Before

Once –
just before
the long skipping rope
hit the ground with a thwack,
I was young.

And days sprawled
indeterminate
and borderless
until the tug of hunger
pulled me home.

No take-aways then,
Only nature's hedgerow treats
sour and sweet on the tongue,
and streams
to drink or suck from icy mittons.

Oh the glory days
of limitless possibility
and no responsibility
and the unrespectability
of climbing trees
and lounging
with your knees apart

And that feeling
just before the rope thwacked,
that 'spring into the line'
'just in time',
and the dip in your knees
ready for the jump
and your heartbeat
racing.

Understanding

"It's just a cup" he says
Baffled by the reverence with which I
lift it to my lips.

"It's more than a cup" I start to say
but then I stop.
It's impossible to explain.

How can I put into words
the bubble of joy that rises as I raise
the cup in my hands?
The happiness that flows through my veins
as the coffee flows over my tongue?

It's only coffee in a cup.

But do you see how the handle
fits my thumb and fingers perfectly?
And how the lip of the cup
is fine although the cup is weighty?
It's a big cup,
I'm in France when I drink from it ,
with a croissant in my hand.
Do you see how the yellow of the handle
is the colour of sunflowers?
And the green round the lip
is like the newest green of spring?
And the patterns of red and blue

are like Spirograph and looking at them
I'm a child again with coloured biros
and plastic wheels and endless days
of possibilities?

See how the pattern round the rim
dances and blurs as I dip
my mouth to kiss the coffee.
Dancing eyes blur when we taste a lover's lips.

It's so much more than a cup.
And I had to look in so many
Tescos and Asdas and Morrisons and Sainsburys
and even charity shops
before I found the right one.
And every morning when I open the cupboard
and see it on the shelf
It makes me excited for the day.
When I heat the milk and add the coffee
I am with Dad again as he teaches me
to boil the milk in the pan.

It's a cup full of memories
It took a lifetime to fill
If you don't understand
I don't think you ever will.

The Blue Hat

I put the blue hat back,
The one that swung from my hand
as I walked to the beach.

I reached up
and found a space
next to a cap that shouted "Greece"
across its brim,
and fitted it in.

And a little part of me
some scent maybe
or a strand of hair
stayed there
upon the shelf,

As the rest of me
placed my feet
once more
upon the ground.

Tracy's She Wee

Now Tracy bought a She Wee
She carried it with pride
Next time she went out walking
she wouldn't have to hide.
She wouldn't have to search for trees
or crouch in the long grass
For she would have her She Wee
in her rucksack on her back!

Well nature came a calling
As Nature always does
And Tracy took her She Wee out
with the minimum of fuss
And as her girlfriends went in search
of hollows and of walls
Tracy got ready to wee wee
whilst standing very tall!

The man said when she bought it
it was easy to fit together
And really would save your modesty
in any kind of weather,
But as she tried in vain to fit
the receptacle to the spout
She stood with legs crossed firmly
but couldn't work it out.

By now her friends had finished
and they came to lend a hand
But even with the four of them
they couldn't understand
how it fitted together
or how it worked it all
So Tracy dropped her walking pants
and weed behind a wall!

With fond memories of Glenn's 50th in the Peak District!

Morning Prayer

I wish you a day filled with living
so sweet – it will move you to tears.

A chorus of birdsong to raise you,
as the misted hills appear.

The gift of another's compassion,
a place in which you are free.

A purpose which always honours you,
all these things may the new day bring.

May your steps be light but steady,
May your thoughts be creative but true,

May your words be clear but gentle
And may love live in all that you do.

Frogs Crossing!

A circular walk around Stocks Reservoir in the Trough of Bowland

Length: 7 miles

Allow 3.5 hours

Parking at the bottom end of the reservoir is free – room for 3 cars only.

Dropping down into Slaidburn from the Ribble Valley, drive to the centre of the village and turn right by the war memorial. Drive 2/3 mile and turn right at the Stocks Reservoir sign. Follow the lane round to the left and once up a little hill you will see a small parking area on the left.

This is the first longer distance walk that I did on my own many years ago and no matter how many times I return to it, whatever the season, it always astounds me that a such a comparatively easy walk, can include such variety, reward you with expansive, lonely views and include a café on the way back!

Parking in the little car park, I turned off the noontime news of Brexit (which is making me and a few million other people feel uncertain, frustrated and anxious) and breathed a sigh of relief as I pulled on my boots and snapped the fastenings on my day-sack. A sign opposite warned me that frogs may be crossing the road and I found myself immediately remembering the excitement of watching for tadpoles in the village water trough when I was little. Checking every day as the frogspawn turned into tadpoles which then grew little legs and one day turned into little green frogs! Brexit well and truly forgotten, I turned right and down the lane I had just driven up. (You can go either way, but I like to have the café at the end of the walk not the beginning.)

The day was perfect for walking. The sun taking the chill off the breeze. Fluffy clouds in a blue sky; a day full of the promise of warmer days to come. The colours of Spring were all around as new leaves unfurled along branches, turning winter brown/black trees to vibrant green and dandelions, daisies and celandines carpeted the verges in bright whites and sunny yellows.

As the lane swung to the right, I took the kissing gate opposite, clearly signed in blue for the circular walk and walked across the bottom of the reservoir. Tiny birds darted ahead of me, a lone fisherman was sitting in a white rowing boat way across the water and to my right, the Bowland Fells were seemingly rolling on forever. At the far side of the reservoir, the path leads left and I followed the shoreline past woods where shadowy glades, that only the birds know about, lay hidden behind the tall firs.

My shadow, which had forsaken me through the winter months, was sticking to my heels again as I followed the path as it undulated across the field. Soon I was opening a tall wooden gate, which is presumably to keep deer out of the newly planted wood. Last time I'd been here, the trees had been felled and it looked like a tsunami had ripped through, creating a desolate landscape. Now, 18 months on, saplings were stretching towards the sky, their tender limbs in protective green tubes. I wondered whether in 30 years or so, when I am gone and the trees are tall and strong, my grandchildren will walk in my footsteps, not knowing that I had witnessed the trees' first springtime, the first buds ripening, the first leaves opening. If so, will they stop on the path, where only glimpses of the water will then be seen between the trees, will they listen to the wind in the branches and peer into the shadows beyond the curving path?

The path leaves the woods and winds across a field and soon you are at the head of the reservoir. It's worth mentioning, that apart from the first 5 minutes of the walk by the reservoir wall, you would never believe that Stocks is a reservoir. It's just as beautiful as the Lake District lakes and once away from the wall at the start, there are no reminders at all that this is an engineered stretch of water.

At the head of the reservoir, the path meanders through established woodland, where mossy tree trunks rest, briars twist and last years leaves return to the soil from whence they came. I breathed in the scent of the woods and the blossom and strode on with tensions loosening and spirits rising. After ten minutes or so, I noticed a little stony beach on my left and followed a narrow path to the shore. Two Canadian geese were gliding, the straight lines of their passage cutting across the ripples on the water. As I approached, they honked noisily and paddled away in perfect symmetry. I stood on the shoreline, surprised at the sea-salty tang that rose from the lapping water. The fells in the distance rose to meet the skyline with their grey-blues and greens and golds and ridges and folds, framing the picture perfect day.

Looking down, I searched for some skimming stones, imagining my Dad crouched behind me, arms around me, his big hands holding my small ones. Then, a flick of his wrist and the stone arching and skimming and skipping faster and faster until it disappeared under the cool blue. Magic memories. I skimmed my stones and didn't disgrace myself. I hope he was watching.

Back to the path and guess what was slowly making its way across? A frog, or it may have been a toad. Anyway, I picked it up, feeling its smooth belly slide across my palm, and set it down in the grass, safe from striding boots.

I was now at the car park at the top of the reservoir (this one is pay and display), and I headed straight across and continued on the path. A lurcher came bounding past me but no master or mistress appeared. I was just beginning to worry, when a second lurcher appeared and behind him, a couple emerged from a path on my right. They started to shout "Benson, Benson." I reassured them that he was ahead of them by some five minutes or so and they hurried on!

After half a mile or so, the path stops following the shoreline and heads off at a 45 degree angle right. (Don't worry, this is the middle part of the walk, which takes you into the Hodder valley and the lower slopes of the fells.) Once out of the woods, the views start to open up as you cross a field which, in June, is a riot of colour, with a carpet of blue, pink, yellow and crimson wild flowers. Down to a little bridge and the path then leads right, up a gentle slope on a well-defined farm track of old. Turning for a breather, I could see Pendle Hill on the far horizon, and the reservoir stretched below me, the water now looking more grey than blue as the clouds moved in. The sun disappeared and it was time to put on my extra fleece and my woolly head band. That East wind was really nippy away from the shelter of the woods. At the top of the track is an old farm where once a farmer whistled his dogs from the barn, but now only the wind whistled through the empty windows and the broken roof. The path goes left in front of the farm and drops down the slope to the River Hodder in the bottom. I tucked myself behind the wall here and ate my lunch. Sipping my hot coffee I heard the gate clang and then an English bulldog with his big wrinkly face came snuffling towards me and my sandwich, "No you don't," I laughed and his owner, who had been lost in the glorious, expansive views, nearly jumped out of his boots! "Oh, I didn't see you there!" he said and we both laughed.

The source of the Hodder is only about 2 miles north of this spot and I got my map out to see if there was a path linking it to this one, but I couldn't find one. I did find an interesting circular walk leading from the car park I'd recently crossed, so that's a new walk to look forward to this Spring.

I finished my lunch, gazing across at the long ridge of Saddle Hill and the lonely valley off to my right, where the only sign of human habitation was a barn high on the hillside. 'Heaven', I thought.

Now down the valley side to the narrow footbridge and across 2 fields, all the time following the posts with their turquoise/blue signs. Along the stone flagged path, saying a silent thank you to whomever laid them across the boggy, tussocky slope. Past the gnarled and twisted Alders, holding tight to their new leaves, snug in their purple grey buds, not quite ready yet to meet the cool April days.

Here on the far side of the reservoir, it felt more like February. The sheep were heavy in lamb whilst at home, lambs were already bounding about; most of the trees were still winter dark and the grass was dry and brittle. The wind rolled down the valley and up my sleeves and I wished I had brought a jacket and gloves!

The track returns to the water's edge and now I was level with the fisherman whom I'd seen at the start of my walk. The afternoon was lengthening and sounds were slowing. Or they were until the fisherman pulled a cord and an outboard engine sputtered into life, taking him to a new spot and maybe more fruitful waters! Past a dozen moored white rowing boats, for now content to bob and sway on the water, but waiting for sails on sunny days.

Along this final stretch, there's a café with a nice terrace, but unfortunately it doesn't open until Easter, so there was no tea and cake for me! Through the café car park and onto the lane turning left and past the memorial garden where trees are planted in memory of loved ones. What a lovely place to rest.

Back at the car, miraculously, it was April again! The wind had died down, the trees were green, a bee was buzzing and the birds were singing.

As I drove back along the lane to the road about Slaidburn, yellow primroses nestled under the hedgerows and if you've read any of my walk descriptions before, you'll know that I'm particularly fond of primroses because they really remind me of my Dad. So my lovely walk, away from the pressures of the world was truly complete.

I turned on the radio and was treated to the slow movement of Shostakovich's 2nd piano concerto and oh my, if you haven't heard this, then put it on your list. It was the perfect way to end the perfect afternoon.

Lifted

A short walk up Pendle Hill in the lovely Ribble Valley.

This is a fairly short walk but it's a stiff climb with amazing views as your reward. Choose a midweek day (not in the holidays) if you can, because otherwise you could be walking in a queue of people!

It's only 3.5 to 4 miles – but allow 2 hours.

Park at Barley car park BB12 9JX - £1 for all day.

Yesterday dawned fine but cloudy and according to the BBC, there was no chance of rain.

I, on the other hand was definitely feeling cloudy with a very high chance of tears (rain), it being four weeks to the day since my lovely Mum died.

A difficult day then and one where I needed some willpower to get outside and walk.

The walking had gone by the wayside a bit, as you can imagine, what with all the arrangements and keeping the business going, but I know how much better I feel out in nature and I also know that I have to keep getting the miles in as I am walking the West Highland Way at the end of May.

I had a client meeting at noon near Skipton, so I needed a walk that would take just a couple of hours, but I also wanted to wake up those calf muscles, so Pendle Hill, just 20 minutes drive away, was a good choice.

Barley car park is mad busy at weekends and during holidays, but at 9am on a Wednesday morning in March, mine was one of only 4 cars there.

Boots on, poles in hand, I set off through the village, admiring the daffodils and the green leaves peeping through on the hedgerows. The old cottages on the roadside are witness to thousands of people each year heading up onto the Pendle Witch Way, but this morning there were only one or two others ahead of me.

The sky seemed low and heavy and trying to lift my mood felt a bit like trying to hold up the sky, but as I turned left just after the garage and walked up the side of the babbling brook, I spotted the first few clumps of primroses and couldn't help but smile remembering the story of my Dad and his potent home-made primrose wine.

Between the ages of 7 and 11 I lived in Newby, a tiny hamlet, near Gisburn in the Ribble Valley. These were idyllic childhood years roaming the fields and lanes all day long in the company of good friends, camping out in the woods on the lower slopes of Pendle hill (the very hill I was walking today) and joining in all the village activities in the Village Hall at Rimington. Halcyon days which I am so thankful for.

Dad enjoyed making home made wine and had started with the kits, but when we moved to the country he got more adventurous and made wine with elderberries, rosehips and finally, his triumph, primroses! He needed about 20 buckets of primroses to make about 4 bottles, so he promised me and 3 friends sixpence (that's 2.5pence now) per bucket. 6d could buy quite a few sweets back then so it seemed a good deal to us. Thankfully there were far more wild primroses back then than now but it was still 2 days of back breaking work toiling up and down the steep banks of the streams! However, the wine was worth it, (I got a little glass), it was like golden nectar and became much talked about. He only ever made it once though and so it became a legendary tale!

Anyway back to my walk up Pendle Hill. You really can't get lost on this walk, it is so well signed and after the first ten minutes or so on a little lane you cross a couple of fields, the great bulk of Pendle looming up ahead of you and turn right round the back of Brown House Farm and then left through a kissing gate. Soon you can choose whether to keep right and climb the many stones steps to the summit or zig zag up the path to the left. I chose to go left as I'm not at my fittest at the moment. At this point I parted company with a lovely lady called Anita whom I'd made firm friends with over the last half a kilometre! Walking does that, you stop to let someone past, end up talking, share anything from just a talk about the weather, to comparing other walks, to getting into some really deep issues. I found myself telling Anita why I was finding it tough

walking today, she ended up giving me a big hug and it really helped. So thank you Anita, if you ever read this, you really started to lift my mood.

It has surprised me how much grief exhausts you. Even though I had been preparing to lose Mum for many months and years, due to her sad decline into dementia, it was still a huge shock. There's a weird feeling also of having somehow lost my roots, now that my second parent has died. I am so lucky I know, to have a wonderful husband, 4 happy, healthy children and a new grand-daughter, but it's the end of an era, the end of being a daughter and it just feels odd. And so, as I made my way up the zig-zags, I found myself really out of breath and had to turn and look at the view many times!

But what a view, 8 miles ahead of me was my own Boulsworth, the hill I climb most regularly as it's on my back doorstep. Over to the East were the fells around Skipton, to the South-west, the sprawl of Nelson, merging into Burnley.

Eventually, the trig was in view and so was Anita, heading towards me from the trig! Another short chat and a fond farewell as she headed off down the zig-zags back to her busy life and three children and her plans to scale Ben Nevis in June and the Canadian

Rockies next year for charity – aren't people just amazing.

At the trig as I patted the top, I had to say "Hello Dad" and "Hello Mum" and I remembered the times they had been with me at that very trig as a child when soggy tomato sandwiches and an apple were our reward for making it to the top. Today after marvelling at the 360 degree view across the Bowland fells, the Yorkshire Dales and the Darwen moors, I tucked myself down behind the stone wall and enjoyed my coffee and a naughty cream egg!

I realised at this point that my mood had really lifted and I set off down the hundreds of steps with a spring in my step. On the way down I chatted to an Indian family whose favourite walk is Haystacks, an Asian family climbing Pendle for the first time, two young lads on a quick hike up and 2 runners with spaniels bounding ahead. How wonderful that walking appeals to so many different people and what a lesson in showing us that we are all the same. The sky was still grey as I retraced my steps back through the village past those same old cottages, but my spirits had lifted. The wind, the birdsong, the babbling brook, the pull in my leg muscles on the steep climb – they had all been reminders that life goes on. Strangers had been kind and nature had been there as it always is, miraculously bringing forth it's buds and blossom each Spring.

Life is a cycle, so get on your bike and ride, push on up the hills, even though your lungs feel like they are bursting and shout with joy as you freewheel down the hills.

Following in the footsteps

A short circular stroll around and through Wycoller near Colne in the East of Lancashire.

This is a nice walk for a Sunday afternoon and as you pass through Wycoller you can stop at the cozy café and have home made soup or tea and cakes! Waterproof boots definitely required. I'm lucky because this walk starts at my front door so it's one I've done in all four seasons but each and every time I marvel at the variety of scenery and the depth of history on this easy ramble.

Approx 5.5 miles

Allow 3 hours if you stop at the café. (Allow 4 if you want to include a walk up Boulsworth).

Park at the end of Hollin Hall Trawden BB8 8TJ near Floats Mill, or if you want to start and end at a good pub, park up at the Trawden Arms BB8 8RU and walk up through the village keeping to the left of the church at the top of the hill.

At the end of all the cottages and the newish mill development (Floats Mill), turn right off the tarmac road onto a narrow lane which leads up to a clutch of houses and follow this round to the left for about half a mile. As the lane forks by a farmhouse, take the right fork past a bungalow and on over the cattle grid.

Keep on the lane which passes in front of the bungalow and crosses the field. Beautiful wild Boulsworth Hill rises a mile away on your left and sheep nibble and stare on the laneside. Bent trees ride the ridge on your right and you can see a dark green forest ahead. Over the cattle grid (gate on right) keep to the left of the farmyard you now enter, and look for a footpath sign over a little stream and up old stone steps which are so pretty but can be slippy.

Someone is currently converting a barn here, into some kind of studio and it looks fabulous – "ooh" I thought – "maybe a nice location for my retreats!"

Pass the cottages and through a gate past another farm and barn conversion and across a small wooden bridge which leads to another gate. Through the gate turn sharp right and follow the path along the field edge. You're only 15 minutes from Trawden now but it feels like you are in the middle of nowhere. I often stop in this field and looking up at Boulsworth,

I slow my breathing right down and say some thank you's to the Universe for allowing me to live in such an amazing place.

About half way along this field start to walk 45 degrees left away from the field edge and head towards a small walkers wooden gate in front of the woods. Don't go through the large gate (right of the little gate). It's always boggy here so watch your step. You're straight into the cool spruce woods with their bright green mossy carpet, the path is clear and straight, but then suddenly you're in a field, surrounded on three sides by the woods, it's a secret field and if you're lucky like I was yesterday, a young red deer will bound out of the reeds not 30 yards from you and bounce away over the tussocks, with it's white tufty back end bobbing up and down!

Stand and drink in the stillness and listen to the wind in the trees.

Watch your footing across this field area, it's often boggy underfoot and very up and down; I find my poles a real help here. Just keep heading straight across.

Back into the woods again, these are denser woods but shafts of sunlight fall through the tall pines and sparkle on hanging dew drops. I shook a branch and laughed as the drops cascaded onto my face and mouth. I licked my lips and tasted the pine!

I've walked through these woods many times over the past 4 years or so and although I know others do too, because of the footsteps I follow, I've never once met anyone in the woods, it's a well kept secret!

Emerging from the woods onto the moorland you often see belted Galloways. These lovely black and white curly coated cows, were bred to thrive on low quality and often boggy pastures in Western Scotland, so they are well suited to Lancashire's wet moorlands! But on this day, the sky is blue with just a few fluffy clouds seemingly balancing on top of Boulsworth and there isn't a belted Galloway in sight!

Through the small wooden gate you'll see the old Roman road which runs the length of Boulsworth and you turn left here onto the track. But before doing so yesterday, I sat myself down on a conveniently placed flat boulder and got my notepad and pen out. When I'm walking, words pour into my head and my poor long suffering dog is used to me sitting and scribbling as I sip my flask coffee. The sun was warm on my face though the wind was sneaking round the corner of the wall, so ten minutes was enough and on we strode.

You now keep on the old Roman road (which today forms part of both the Bronte Way and the Pennine Bridleway) for a couple of miles. The views across left to Ingleborough and Pen-y-ghent are spectacular on a clear day and if you are feeling full of energy and you want to see for 40 miles or more in every direction, you can climb up Boulsworth. Just follow the concrete track off to the right just past the first farm you come to, it's a steep climb and you need to bear right on the top to reach the trig. Once at the trig, after drinking in the glorious views, go back along the ridge for half a mile or so and then drop back down near huge boulders, leading you eventually back onto the lane (add on an hour for this).

But yesterday, I kept to the lane, stopping for a second time to write a poem (Stone), sitting on my woolly hat on a stack of round fence poles leaning against a sun warmed barn wall. Another cup of coffee and some flap jack shared with the dog and I was off again. Keep straight on - don't turn left through a gate where the lane leads to a farm, go straight on up a slight rise (there's a wooden signpost here which I think says Wycoller 2 miles) and the lane now becomes an old stone flagged path. This part of the walk is just you and the wild, no farms, no sign of human habitation other than the dry stone wall on your left. Just the hill and a stream in the bottom and ferns and the odd sheep. After 20 mins or so you'll reach a newer man made path which leads you round to the left and into Wycoller Valley. Keep on this path over the big wooden bridge and the rushing stream and stay on this for another half a mile. Eventually the path becomes a clear lane again and at this point there is a farm gate and stile on your left and a path/lane leading down into Wycoller Valley. Take this path which soon leads you past a farmhouse where you join a lane proper with a rushing stream on your left. This is Wycoller Water and some of the oldest stone bridges in Lancashire pass over it. 15 mins now and you're in Wycoller with it's fascinating ruins and bridges and the lovely café I mentioned at the start. The ruins are Wycoller Hall, famed for being regularly visited by the Bronte sisters. In fact, a picture of the Hall was used on the front cover of the 1898 edition of Jane Eyre.

After your café stop you've 2 choices. Either follow the tarmac lane out of the village to the car park and then turn left on the road, picking up the signs for Trawden and entering Trawden just 100 yards left of the pub, or turn left out of the café and look for a lane 50 yards on your right . Walk up here about 5 mins or so and look for a path slightly right into a wood up wooden edged steps.

A bit of a climb here straight through the woods and then over 3 stiles and 3 fields

picking up a lane to Germany Farm. Round the RHS of the farm and through a really boggy bit and over another field. Just go straight across and head for a converted farm ahead slightly right. Through a metal gate with the converted farm in front of you and immediately left down a little snicket to another stone stile. The path is clear and you drop down the left of a large field with two copses of trees inside stone walls, one on your left and one on your right. Pendle Hill is ahead of you and Trawden in the valley bottom below. At the end of the field you emerge bottom left through a small wooden gate and take the lane left down to Foulds Mill.

As I said at the start of this piece, I feel blessed to have walking like this right on my doorstep. Daily, I can walk in countryside unchanged for hundreds of years, in the footsteps of so many; from Roman soldiers following orders, to the Bronte sisters challenging the patriarchal society of the 19th century. Whatever changes and challenges we face, nature doesn't judge, it remains constant and it accepts you as you are. It's where I can truly be me. No make-up, comfy clothes, no rush, no conversations either inside my head or out. Just a sense of being at one with nature, feeling the stones under my feet and the wind on my face. Heaven.

Amazing Day

A walk in the Southern Yorkshire Dales, on the edge of the Ribble Valley.

An easy ramble, mainly on lanes from long ago, with lovely long reaching views of the Skipton Fells and the Dales.

Approximately 6.5 miles

Allow 3 hours

Park on the free car park in Hellifield. BD23 4HT

Yesterday, I had work to do and I dutifully went into my office at 9am and started to pull everything together I needed to write a long report. After a while I looked at the blue sky outside and suddenly thought, "What the hell am I doing? It's Sunday! This is exactly how I got ill nearly 3 years ago, why am I slipping back into these bad habits? For slipping I have been and as a result the anxious feeling is creeping in alongside the headaches and the waking at night. How can I hold myself up as an example to stressed individuals if I'm not practicing what I preach? So I closed my laptop and packed up my rucksack.

It was already 10.30am, so I needed to walk somewhere fairly local and only for 3 – 4 hours. Pouring over my OS Explorer map, I spotted a short walk I'd done in October 2017 which I'd thoroughly enjoyed and I saw that I could add a couple of miles by starting off in Hellifield, only 5 miles from Gisburn.

There's a handy free car park behind the Black Horse pub in Hellifield and across the road is a cozy café (Hazy Dayz) with sofas and a log burner. Realising that I was starving as I'd only had a coffee at home, I had half an hour with the paper and an extremely good full English! Then it was boots on, poles in hand and off up Haw Drive opposite the church.

I passed the terraced houses with Christmas trees all aglow and was soon on Haw Lane, which starts just past the railway line. You have to cross the track so stop and have a good listen for trains. Within minutes, I was in the midst of fields and there were the views I love of old barns and woods, sheep dotted fields and dry stone walls; I could feel the tension in my shoulders starting to ease as I breathed in the cold fresh air. There were deep puddles on the track and in them, the magical upside-down world of reflection. In the large puddle ahead, I could see the trees I had just walked passed, it felt like future, past and present were merged into one glorious moment and reminded me that I'd been missing the moments lately as I raced through the busy lead up to Christmas.

So I stood; noticing the red berries on the tangled tree to my left, the caw-cawing of the rooks circling the field ahead, the distant sound of gun shots on the Skipton Moors and I breathed the November smells of funghi and wet leaves.

An old lady approached on the track, hunched over and walking slowly with a stick; but there she was with her walking boots on about half a mile out of the village. She smiled and talked about the weather, as walkers do and I prayed that I will still be walking at her age. At the end of the track, a gate leads into a field that slopes up to the right, and I kept to the left of the slope heading for the woods straight across. Big broad faced sheep looked at me for a few seconds before they resumed their nibbling.

Crossing a small beck, I headed for a gate which leads onto Dacre Lane. I turned right and followed the track between nature's Christmas trees on the left and gnarled hawthorns, ash and elm on my right. Their bare branches waited patiently behind a green mossed wall, for next summer's show of dancing leaves and choruses of bird song. Along the lane came a farmer on a quad bike, with 2 sheep dogs bounding happily behind, he tipped his cap at me as I stood 'neath the pines, breathing in the lovely sappy scent.

I was soon dropping down into the picture postcard tiny village of Otterburn with its scattering of houses and farms running alongside Otterburn beck. Left and over the stone bridge and then immediately left following the beck-side. You have to go through some big metal gates here and you feel like you are going into someone's private gardens, but you are in fact walking through a farmyard and it is a footpath. Straight past the farm buildings and on to a track (don't go left through a little gate onto the beck side), which I followed for a few hundred yards before

coming to a gate on my right where a footpath sign points left to Kirkby Malham. I looked back at the water crashing around boulders, way higher than last time I'd done this walk and noticed two ponies stood on the crest of the hill opposite, a black and a cream one standing perfectly still. I stood in the sunshine for 2 or 3 minutes and they never moved, a lesson in stillness.

Turning from my shadow and the fast flowing brook, I headed through the gate and made for a copse of trees slightly uphill to my left. Skirting the trees I headed for the gate ahead and I sloshed my way through the mud and strode straight across the next field. Not much sign of a path here but there's a stile straight ahead with a little wooden gate on top of it. Once over this, I kept to the wall, (don't go through an open gateway on the right). At the end of the wall, just keep walking straight across the field. Now you're out on your own proper, just hills and woods and old barns and your shadow to keep you company (plus the sheep of course!) I looked behind and there was majestic Pendle far away under a hazy sun, whilst ahead were the most southerly of the Yorkshire Dales hills. This is a big field, but just keep going straight and you will drop down to a country lane, head for the gate onto the lane and there's a stile ten yards or so to the right of it. This is Scosthrop Lane, go left for a hundred yards or so and then left onto Green Lane where a signpost says Long Preston 3.5 miles.

I had to really march on now, I'd spent so much time taking pictures and making notes that it was already 1.45 and I was only half way round the walk. Not wanting to get caught in the dusk on Crake Moor, I seriously picked up speed. As the track dips there's a couple of deserted cottages at Orms Gill and here I followed a path left down the side between the old deserted cottage and more modern farm buildings.

This next part really doesn't have a clear path at all, I just headed down through the gate past a field barn and through another gate down the field and slightly to the left of a new plantation of trees, across the ford – which was like a river after all the rain so I just had to run through it! Straight up and over the field, keeping Houber woods on your left. Then you eventually come to a wall with no gateways or stiles but don't worry! Keeping the wall in front of you walk upwards and to the right (I think there was another gate here) and at the top of the field is a gateway and some kind of remains of an old farm building, go left through this gate and a track appears in the field in front of you. I had, in fact, after consulting my map again, asked the Universe to send me a sign here; I knew I had to get beyond the woods

to find the lane but where on earth was the path? Sure enough, once through the gate, a track just appeared from nowhere! Follow the track down (woods still on left of you) and at the bottom of the field hey presto, you are back on Dacre lane! So now you just have to retrace your steps by crossing straight over the lane and through the gate into the field, over the little beck, right-ish and along under the sloping side of the field back to Haw Lane. I breathed a big sigh of relief I can tell you when I found I was back on Dacre Lane. My map reading skills are good, but you don't want to be in the middle of nowhere on a December afternoon after 3 o clock. Always aim to be down from the fells by 2.30 on a winter afternoon.

Now I was back on the home straight, I looked for a through-stone in a wall as it was too wet to sit on the grass and I had a perch for 5 minutes and a well deserved cup of coffee and a biscuit. I recalled that last time I did this walk I struggled with the path too, but that time I'd stayed on Green Lane until I got to Crake Moor Farm and the farmer who just so happened to be passing in his land-rover, told me to go through his farm yard, go through the gate by the silage bails on the left, then just follow the wall all the way down to the beck and head for the part of the moor ahead where it was brown on one side and green on the other! He was right and this brought me onto an earlier section of Dacre Lane. I often find that when I am trying to find a missing footpath, some-one will appear, a lone walker or a farmer to reassure me that I am on the right route. And, if all else fails, you can always turn around and retrace your steps!

I was soon back into Hellifield and in the car for 3.40. It had been a walk of muddy tracks and puddles, fields and moorland and woods, hazy sun and blue-grey skies and I'd not given work or anything else much a thought. Looking for the next gate or stile, checking your map, soaking up the views and breathing in all that cold fresh air, is a wonderful way to ease those shoulders and dissolve that knot at the top of your stomach. Which is why when I add today's walk to my calendar, I will have walked 800 miles so far this year. I am trying to get to 1000 miles in one year and I promise I will in 2019!

Back in the car, I turned the stereo on to find Coldplay playing 'Amazing Day' and thought how fitting that Chris was singing about how I felt at that exact moment.

'And I asked every book
Poetry and chime
Can there be breaks
In the chaos of times?
Oh, thanks God
You must've heard when I prayed
Because now I always
Want to feel this way

Amazing day
Amazing day.'

© *Amazing Day. Coldplay, Universal Music Publishing Group, 2015.*

Grimwith Reservoir

A good walk for newbies to walking alone, as you are never far from civilization and there's an option to walk either 4 or 8 miles. Allow 4 to 4.5 hours.

The walk takes you around Grimwith Reservoir near Burnside in the Yorkshire Dales and then over towards Appletreewick and is on good paths and bridleways. There are delightful views throughout, even though the walk involves little climbing.

Parking – drive to Burnsall and then take the B6265 towards Pateley Bridge. After a mile look for a sign to Hebden on the RHS, turn down and park after about 100 yds on the right near Beck House.

Refreshments and toilets at Burnsall and also a lovely café at Hebden in the converted schoolrooms – gluten free cakes to die for. Other than that plenty of walls and ferns ladies!

I always plan my walks ahead and photocopy the area of the OS Explorer map that I need. I mark out the walk and leave a copy for Glenn (hubby) so that if I fail to materialize he'll know where to send the search party. I know you can get maps on your phone but although I always have my phone on me, I hate looking at it when I'm walking. I walk to escape the trappings of the modern world. I also like being able to read a map and believe it is a skill fast becoming forgotten as people rely more and more on GPS. So armed with the photocopy in a plastic cover (as it can always rain!) and with the full map and a compass in my day sack, I'm ready for off.

I feel excited as I drive towards a walk I haven't done before and yesterday, with a decent day forecast, I was heading towards Burnsall and feeling like a happy bunny!

Slipping my feet into my walking boots feels like coming home and rucksack on and poles in hand, I'm ready to conquer the world, well a few miles of it anyway!

Up to the main road and straight across onto Hartlington Moor Lane, a rough but good track between those familiar Yorkshire stone walls. A bright day with cotton wool clouds, patches of blue and some heavy grey; with a westerly breeze keeping the temperature around 13 degrees, a typical August day then! Waterproofs in my sack just in case, but soon the fleece was off and tied round my middle as I stretched my legs up the gentle incline, heading towards the reservoir. Soon a red admiral joined me, alighting on mottled stones and dancing across the lane in front of me. Splashes of pink willowherb nestled amongst thistle and nettle on the lane-side and the green hills of the Dales rolled on in every direction.

After a mile or so the reservoir came into view on my right, the water so low that there it only seemed to cover about half the bottom, but still a handful of sailboats were out and with the sun sparkling on the water, it was an arresting sight. Joining the reservoir circular path, I walked past spruce woods, breathing in the crisp smell of pine and hearing the fain coo of a wood-pigeon; and on past boulder strewn beaches that are usually submerged in the deep deep waters of the reservoir.
 Across two quaint old fashioned wooden bridges with Blea Beck tumbling down from Grassington Moor, frothing around rocks and boulders and rushing, peaty brown towards the reservoir. In my stride now, passing 2 couples

with 2 dogs – except one of the dogs was missing. "Poppy", "Poppy", they were yelling and then there was the sound of crashing and panting in the waist high ferns near me and I shouted "I think she's here!" Sure enough a black spaniel, full of bits of bracken and seeds came bounding out, looking very happy, having had a great adventure in a big tall jungle!

As you walk round the reservoir, interesting looking paths veer off to the left, but none are signposted or indeed showed up on my map, so I stuck to the waterside.

The sails boats sailed, their crew leaning far out over the water and the sun warmed my face and sparkled on the water and my boots crunched the gravel. All was well with the world.

At the bottom (or maybe it's the top) of the reservoir, is a 400 year old cruck barn with its heather thatch roof restored to its original glory. Evidently all the barns in the Dales used to be like this, with very steep roofs supported by wooden crucks on top of the stone sides, but there are literally a handful left. I stood and wondered who had farmed there in the 1600s when the barn was built, long before there was a reservoir, a wild and hard life maybe.

The last leg of the circuit takes you through tall marsh woundwort, their pink flowers and feathery white soft seeds reminding me of candyfloss at the fair.

Up now to the car park and out to the left picking up a good track across fields to the B6265, past wide eyed sheep who were content to stare as I walked merely feet from them.

Straight across the road (you could go right here and back to your car if you just want to walk 4 miles) the path leads on and into more fields, with the jagged outline of Burhill Ridge on your left and some rocky outcrops just begging to be climbed nearer to hand. Worth a scramble to sit on the top and dangle your legs whilst you eat a sandwich!

The path joins New Road (a tarmacked road) for about a hundred yards or so and then leaves the road to the right on a clearly marked bridleway, signposted to Hartlington. Now you're on farmed land with sheep a plenty and gorgeous brown cows chewing. Beautiful views of Barden Fell and Burnsall and Thorpe Fell surround you, in fact you can see for miles. Way over to the wind turbines beyond Burnley left and far beyond Malham over to your right. A good place to sit and write a poem (*see page opposite*), whilst I had a coffee and my other sandwich. Soft grass for my cushion and a stone wall for my back – heaven!

Dropping down past farm buildings, sounds drifting up the valley from Burnsall where there was a Bank Holiday weekend sports day event in progress.

Down and down, past Hartlington Hall, a beautiful old hall nestling in woodland and eventually to the tiny road in the valley bottom where I realised as I turned right, past picture post-card cottages, that I would now need to climb all the way back up the valley side to my car! Still, I'd done little climbing during the whole walk and so pushed on past converted barns and cottages and farms. I wondered if their occupants woke up every day and looked at the views and wondered how they ever got to be so lucky.

A rider on an amazing grey trotted past with a cheery hello and a tractor had me climbing into the nettles as it missed me by about 6 inches but I made it back to the car unscathed and filled with the joys of living.

Four and a half hours of breathing in the beauty of the Dales does that for you.

Now

Now to the boulders and the straight stone walls
The sharp escarpment and the wind-bent tree,
The peat stained waterfalls of coffee and cream
where the bracken curls and the heather clings.

Wide skies hold the promise of everything
from cotton—cloud Summer to
sharp showery Spring,
Patches of blue midst rolling grey
A 'fleece on, fleece off' kind of day.

Now from the bracken to the sheep-neat grass
The rusted gate and the farmland track,
Down past the hall on the old stone path
Where history hides its secret past.

Deep in the valley the river runs
Stars explode as sunlight falls,
Silent now, I stand enthralled
Lost and found in the wonder of it all.

The first T shirt day of the year!

A walk that starts high up, so you've got the views right from the get-go plus it's impossible to get lost – well almost!

5.5 miles – allow 2.5 hours.

Parking 2 miles along the road from Embsay near Skipton, to Barden, small car park marked on the map as Black Hill. BD23 6AR.

There were blue skies stretching as far as the eye can see as I drove from home to Skipton last Friday and I couldn't wait to get out into the fresh but nippy air. Taking the minor road sign-posted to Barden from Embsay village, I was soon climbing up onto the moor tops with Wharfedale in all its glory stretching in front of me.

I was looking for a car park named Black Hill, but nothing was appearing, so when I got the to the top and there was a flat area with several cars parked, I thought that must be it! (I now know it wasn't and I should have been 200 yards further on! Over the brow of the hill in fact.) However, there was a signpost opposite which seemed to tie in with the instructions in my Cicerone walking guide, so I strode off across the moors. Sometimes, it just feels wrong. Though the path was clear, I felt I should be going straight and I was soon veering left and after 15 mins I was at a trig, (which I now know was High Crag). "Ah well," I thought, "It's beautiful and I've got all afternoon, I'll do a bit of exploring." So I sat down by the trig and drank in the view whilst I drank my coffee and I had a good look at the lay of the land.

Standing with my back to where I'd left the car, Upper and Lower Barden Reservoir were to the right of me and Hellifield Cragg was over to my left at about 45 degrees. The walk I'd planned had been around the two reservoirs and I could see the very clear track leading up and around them. I figured I could continue on my path to the left and circle round, ending up eventually on the reservoir track. I'd got my map and a path ahead of me, so off I went.

The path meandered across the moor top towards a small wood, a red admiral flitted about in front of me, the sky was porcelain blue and looked liked a massive china dinner plate with a swirling edge of haze. Tiny pink flowers covered the heather and the wind whistled through the pines. The path followed the side of the wood and eventually dropped all the way down into a little valley following a wall. It was a well used path, plenty of boot-prints which always makes you feel like you're not lost (even if you're not on the walk you're supposed to be on!).

Across a little stream the path continued up the other side but I was still heading left away from the reservoirs, in fact I seemed to be heading towards Embsay Cragg, which I'm sure is a lovely walk but not for today. So I branched off the path across the moors, heading for a track and a line of shooting huts I could see on my map. Down another steep little valley, glad of my poles, across a tumbling beck and up the other side on hands and knees (!) and sure enough after another ten minutes of following my nose, there was the track and the shooting huts. Phew! This stretch would have been really boggy in winter, but after a spell of mostly fine weather, it was just lovely and soft and springy. The track soon joined a broader track which was the one I should have been on all along which sets off on Black Hill Car-park. Turning left towards Lumb Gill Head, I was soon fascinated by the sight of Mr and Mrs Moorhen who were engaged in some kind of complicated courting routine.

Mr Moorhen, with his red crown and distinctive 'bedump' call which crescendoed into a really fast repeating 'wick,wick,wick,wick as he trotted after Mrs Moorhen who was having none of him, was both endearing and hilarious to behold. She was tripping over the heather and everytime he nearly caught up, off she went again. All this was happening about 15 feet away from me, it was such good fun to watch, I felt like I was in an episode of Springwatch on BBC! (Other nature programmes and channels available!)

After twenty minutes or so of walking, looking down towards the sparkling waters of Barden High Reservoir, a path led off downhill to the right and there, by a boulder was a rabbit, so intent on nibbling the new spring grass, that I literally crept within 6 feet of him. I slowly got

my phone out ready to take a photo, but could only see his body and the tips of his ears, so I was carefully creeping round the back of the boulder when he suddenly tensed, ears pricked; then he was away, running between the heather and bracken, soon lost to view.

Dropping down to the reservoir, past more courting moorhens, I could see and hear (!) hundreds of seagulls swooping and diving over the water. What a racket. I couldn't decide whether this was also Spring madness or just that so many of them lived there but I'd never heard so many caw-cawing together.

At this point on my walk, my jacket was already off and in my back-pack, but now a momentous thing happened. The sun was shining and for the first time in 2019, the fleece top also came off and there I was in my cotton short-sleeved shirt. Oh, how good the sun on my white arms felt. It was still breezy, so I had a woolly head-band on, but my arms were swinging in the sunshine and all was well. Next thing you know, I'll be rolling my trousers up!

The path now lead across the bottom of the reservoir, towards a striking Victorian house, long empty. I tried to imagine the family living there in the 1890's, in the middle of nowhere, the father employed as the reservoir keeper, who had to operate the various sluices and gates by hand. What joy in summer, but how remote in the winter-time with no phone or car.

After a short stop for my lunch I followed the path to the right (just past the house, by the wooden signpost.) In fact, it's a bit confusing here, don't follow the first track to the right, keep going until you are by the wooden signpost. Here, you can continue straight on, eventually walking all the way to Burnsall, if you fancy it and then you can pick up the Dales Way back to Barden Bridge and walk back the last mile or so along the road to the car park. A nice walk for a summer afternoon methinks.

The track curves around the valley side and down toward Barden Lower Reservoir. Ahead were fields and woods, across, patchwork squares of sludgy greens and every shade of brown, stretching for miles across the moorland. I stood by a tiny brook and marveled at how still and clear the water was where the land was flat and how when the land dropped, the water fell so quickly, noisily frothing and splashing until the land leveled again. I thought about how life is like the water in a stream, sometimes it's calm because everything is on the level and then the ground under your feet drops away when you are least expecting it and you fall fast and crash about trying to feel the bottom, until, a little further on, the frothing and splashing becomes less and

there's just a few bubbles and the water calms again as you reach another smooth place.

The wind was gentle, the sun was dancing on the reservoir; nature was working its magic again, my soul was soothed, my mind was emptied, my breathing was deep and the kinks in my neck and shoulders were ironing themselves out.

After twenty minutes or so, and just before the lower reservoir, I followed a path that dips down off to the right into tiny little valley and crosses the stream just before the reservoir. It then winds its way back up to the road and it was at this point that I realised this was supposed to be where I parked! I walked the last half mile with a friendly young guy from Newcastle who enthralled me with his tails of walking many of the long distance trails in France and Spain. I left him at his car and carried on up the hill on the road, not entirely sure how much further I had left to walk. But just over the cattle grid and round the bend, there was my red Alfa.

A wonderful walk then, where I followed my nose, studied my map with a baffled look in my eye, watched courting dances, got the sun on my winter-white arms, had a nice chat and rejoiced once again in the therapeutic effects of nature.

Boots off, back in the car. I watched the antics of a human courting couple, who'd parked next to me. She was running ahead of him across the grass and posing as he took photos of her with his phone. They were both laughing and as they got back in the car, he leaned over and kissed her. I wondered if Mr Moorhen ever managed to catch and kiss his lady friend?

Smiling I drove back down the country road into Embsay, where there is a lovely pub called the Elm Tree. Next time, I thought!

On top of the world

A walk to Simon's Seat above Bolton Abbey

A lovely varied walk on clear paths so it's suitable for winter or summer walking with a lovely café at the beginning or end!

Approx 8.5miles

Allow 3.5 – 4 hours

Parking at Bolton Abbey (park in the village as it costs £10 to park at the actual abbey) BD23 6EX

Waking on a Sunday in mid February, I wasn't sure what the day was going to bring, it was all looking a bit murky and grey out of the bedroom window, but when I checked the BBC weather forecast for the Skipton area, sunny intervals were forecast from lunchtime onwards, so I got the maps out! I quite fancied picking up the Dales way at Flasby – I love those low and rolling hills and valleys, but I really needed an OS explorer map of the area as the one I have is a Landranger one I picked up by mistake and as such, the detail isn't great for walking.

Still intending to walk above Flasby, I packed up the rucksack with a nice Lancashire cheese and pickle butty and my customary flask of coffee and set off via Skipton, where I bought the requisite map. Next to the maps were the walking route books and so I treated myself to 'Walking in the Yorkshire Dales – South and East' by Dennis and Jan Kelsall, which I had a quick look through over a cuppa. The walk up to Simon's seat above Bolton Abbey looked interesting and was a new one for me so I decided to leave Flasby for another day.

Parking the car on the wide banks of the River Wharfe at Bolton Abbey and reeling from the shock of having to pay £10 for the privilege(!) I booted up and set off over the bridge by the Cavendish Pavilion café which holds fond memories for me as my god-daughter's wedding reception was held there 2 years ago. Sunny memories in both senses of the word.

The path leads upwards through woods (not along the river) to a lane where you take a left for a couple of hundred meters until you reach a gate on the right by a pretty cottage. A clear track leads across the fields as the swell of Brown Hill and South Nab rise on your right. Immediately I was away from the busier paths of Bolton Abbey and on my own – although I'm sure there will be more people around in the summer. A stream gurgles away in a ravine on the left and old oak trees with twisted limbs watch you on your way. It's a gradual sloping path winding its way along through what is called the Valley of Desolation – but there's nothing desolate about it! Evidently in 1826 flash floods stripped the valley bare but now it's quiet beautiful; woods sprawl along the sides and the beck splashes its way down waterfalls and around the boulders, peat dark and frothy cream like an Irish coffee.

The sun was trying to break through and I was boiling in the quilted down jacket my husband had bought me for Christmas, a lovely thought, but I am never cold these days – even in mid winter, so it was soon in my rucksack and I suspect it will spend most of its future in there! Over the beck, the stony path winds up-wards and soon I was in the woods where a sign-post points clearly ahead to Simon's Seat. I stood for a moment, watching a couple of blue-tits chasing each other from tree to tree and listening to their happy song. Shadows were falling long onto the path and a fallen pine tree lay amongst the winter bracken, its moss covered branches soft and green against the brown and brittle fronds.

Up through the woods and soon the moors were stretching far and wide in front of me. On through a kissing gate and straight ahead (a path goes off to the left here but ignore this). Now the moors were all around and the path was clearly visible arching its way and climbing ahead left in front of me. This is my kind of heaven, moorhens calling, wind in the long grass, the path changing from mud, to boulder, to crunching stone so that you have to watch each step; it's impossible to think about everyday worries when you're concentrating on your footing or stopping to drink in the views. It's quite a pull up and around the wide flank of the moor and great boulders, dumped unceremoniously by a million year old glacier, sit in silence, watching over you as you plod along, breathing hard, working those calf muscles. Great Agill Beck tumbles down from Great Agill Head on your left, buzzards wheel in the wide skies and dark and tangled heather carpets the land. Eventually, the path crosses a

series of small tributaries and makes its way left across Nanny Crag. Quite an appropriate name I thought, as I will become a Nanny for the first time very soon!

Reaching a crooked T junction you take a right and as I did, a couple approaching me smiled and said , "Not far now". I wondered if I looked knackered? I didn't feel it! The final half a mile or so to the trig is on rough terrain, picking your way over small boulders and avoiding muddy puddles, up and down over peaty tussocks - probably a lot easier in the summer months. But my poles come in handy on stretches like this and I was soon on the approach to the massive pile of boulders which is Simon's Seat and that familiar white trig. Leaving my rucksack and poles, I clambered up, finding footholds in narrow crevices and crawling onto the huge boulders. It was really windy at the top so I had to hold on to the trig, but heaven was stretching in every direction. The sky was grey and blue and white and the Yorkshire hills stretched on for ever, in every direction. Surely one of the most stunning views in the Dales. I really felt like I was on top of the world. "Another one Dad" I said, placing my palm flat down on the trig.

I hunkered down out of the wind and had a well-deserved cup of flask coffee and let the beauty of the landscape sooth my soul as the coffee cup warmed my hands.

The descent starts on a flagged path to the South West and as it was already 3pm, I reluctantly made my way away from the incredible vantage point and vowed to return in the Spring when the days would be longer. The path winds across the moor and descends hugging the side of High Brown Hill; the views across Wharfedale to Burnsall and beyond are simply gorgeous. After half a mile or so, you reach Upper Fell Plantation, and the path leads through tall pines where the wind was singing in the branches and joins a wider track where you keep right and descend to Howgill lane. Go straight across the lane down a narrow path and soon you are in the valley bottom with the River Wharfe flowing wide and strong in front of you. The path now leads left downstream for a mile or so to Barden Bridge. It was now approaching 4pm and the sun had taken on that golden hue so often seen at the end of a fine winter's day. It bathed the valley sides, turning the heather orange-gold, brightening the green of the sheep-cropped meadows and sparkling on the river. All was well in my world.

At Barden Bridge, the ruins of Barden Hall stood proud, her crumbling walls holding on to secrets of battles won and lost. Her vacant windows, where Lord Clifford once gazed at stars, bear silent witness to love and loss and life and death and the passing of the seasons which all too soon merge into years and centuries.

Time was marching on for me too and I therefore chose the quickest route back to Bolton Abbey on the far side of the bridge. (You can also take the path on the near side of the bridge which takes you up higher and affords splendid views.)

As I walked back through Strid woods, the Wharfe narrowed, the water swirled and crashed and fell between the dark rocks; the deep underwater currents and rocks here are lethal and walkers are warned to keep well back and never ever attempt to jump across. It's a deadly kind of beautiful, it looks like a narrow beck, but several people have slipped into these waters and died. I kept well back and hurried along as the light was fading and the path is tricky in places. The woods are steep sided and as the last of the sunlight danced through the branches and dappled the path in front of me, I breathed in the smells of sap and moss and last years leaves and thanked the Universe for allowing me to experience valleys and streams and woods and moors and rivers and lanes and birdsong and smiles and wind and sunshine and excitement and caution and wonder and happiness all in the space of three hours. And apart from the cost of the car park, which I could have avoided if I'd done this walk from

Barden Bridge instead of Bolton Abbey, all of this incredible experience hadn't cost me a bean!

A Walk on the Wild Side

A walk through the valleys and farmlands of Glusburn and Crosshills near Skipton.

Approximately 6.5 miles

Allow 3 hours

Heading East on the A6068 towards Crosshills, turn left at the first sign for Ickornshaw, after 50 metres or so, there is room to park 3 or 4 cars on your right.

BD22 0DH

Saturday started with long intervals of sunshine and it appeared that the forecasters may be wrong and that the rain yet again, would not arrive.

So, washing on the line and work done, I got out my map and decided where to trek.

As I made my flask of coffee and sandwich, some clouds appeared, but there was still plenty of sunshine around. I popped my waterproofs in my day sack just in case and looked forward to a good long walk.

My plan was to park up at at Ickornshaw, only five miles from home and pick up the Pennine way to Lothersdale and beyond and then circle back Cononley way, walking nine or ten miles. There's a handy roadside pull in as you turn down into Ickornshaw off the A6068 and lucky for me there was room for just one more car. So boots on and map tucked into my front pocket and I was off.
Ickornshaw is a tiny village, with a jumble of cottages lining the steep little road, a converted old mill, a stream running behind, pretty gardens and little snickets here and there leading to leafy lanes and hidden houses. The Pennine way drops down into the village on wooden edged steps and crosses the road over the stream. Picking up the way-marked sign, I turned left into a lane leading between cottages, past a bungalow where flowers spilled over the walls and on towards a working farm.

The sun was warm and soon my fleece was off and my water bottle was in hand. As I crossed the fields, cows calmly chewed and I started to relax as nature worked its magic. Past farms, down narrow lanes and along a stream side path, where the sun filtered through an archway of branches and butterflies danced between the foxgloves.

Now for the first climb up Cowling Hill and my calves reminded me that I hadn't been doing enough walking lately, oh how they burned! But soon I was on the hill top and the long views towards the Yorkshire Dales opened up. The skies were wide and blue ahead but behind me skies were steely and to the East, showers fell in soft bands of grey. The wind whipped my hair across my face and I laughed at the force of it.

Down into Lothersdale and a short stop for half a Thatchers and some Yorkshire crisps, the sun still keeping those clouds at bay. Then leaving the Pennine Way, I walked up Tow Top Lane, enjoying the long and familiar views of hills and dry stone walls. The weather was definitely changing, the blue skies heading away from me now and clouds behind rolling in from the East. The fleece was back on as I checked my map and considered whether it would be wise to visit the pretty village of Cononley and climb Gott Hill beyond. The skies behind me were menacing and Boulsworth hill looked like it was already getting a soaking, so I resigned myself to cutting my walk short and headed for Street Head farm and started to drop down Cononley Moor on a well defined track. Lucky for me, as the first rain shower hit me, I'd just reached the corner of the field where, tucked down near the bottom of the wall, was a through stone protruding just far enough for me to perch on. Hood up and coffee poured, I watched the rain pelt the parched ground.

It was a short shower and I was soon on my way again, stripping off the layers and rolling up my walking trousers as I headed back towards Crosshills, with Gib Side and the old mine workings opposite. Wishing I had time to wander up and explore but knowing I'd had to leave this for another day, I pushed on trying to beat the worsening weather which was now moving in quickly. Past the converted farms and barns of Ley House and down to the ford. Feeling the temperature drop, I made my way up through the wooded bridleway, no sunlight filtering through the leaves now; all felt dark and eerie. Only a mile and a half now back to the car and I thought I might just beat the rain. But as the path leveled and I headed across the fields to Long Lane, I heard the first

rumble of thunder and rain swept across the tops. Quickly pulling on my waterproofs and covering my day-sack, I sat on a grassy tussock behind a wall and tucked myself into the side of a holly bush, balancing my rucksack on my knee to keep my feet as dry as possible. (*The next pages show my writing from that day.*)

And so, down into Ickornshaw, past the farm where an old tractor rusted and a sheep dog barked. Past the school, with upturned chairs on tables in an empty classroom, past the cottages with hanging baskets dripping and the lane running like a river. Smelling the freshness, the heady scent of flowers and the sharp smell of the stone walls and people emerging from their cottages into the newness of the rain.

Back to the car and the modern world, exhilarated and thankful for another walk, a walk on the wild side.

Near Lotherdale
hunkered down behind
the old wall
I watched the wild
now enfold

Gone were the blue sky
& gentle her
Now all was grey
& lightning
grey & wet & loud
as the skies poured
down weeks of rain

And the lightning
cracked, &
Thunder rolled as
I counted the

28/7/18
seconds
close, close still,
& me hunkered
down behind the
drystone wall

In the midst
& fury of it all.

Now overhead —
& hailstones pelted
the puddles
& the trees swayed
in glorious
confusion as the
wind rocked &

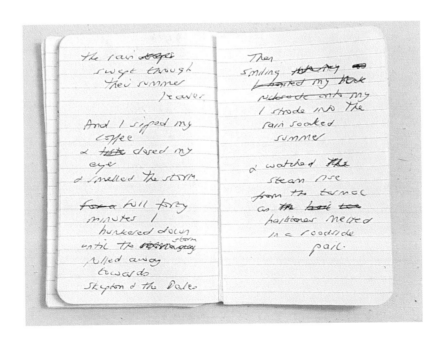

the rain
swept through
their summer
leaves.

And I sipped my
coffee
& closed my
eye
& smelled the storm.

For a full forty
minutes I
hunkered down
until the storm
rolled away
towards
Skipton & the Dales

Then
smiling my
my
I strode into the
rain soaked
summer

& watched the
steam rise
from the tarmac
as the
hailstones melted
in a roadside
pail.

Hunkered down behind the old wall
I watched the wildness unfold.
Gone were the blue skies and gentle breeze,
Now all was grey and wet and loud
as the skies poured down weeks of rain.
And the lightening cracked
and the thunder rolled
as I counted the seconds,
Close, closer still.

And me, hunkered down behind the dry-stone wall
in the midst and fury of it all.

Now – overhead.
Hailstones pelted the puddles
and trees swayed in glorious confusion
as the wind roared and the rain swept
through their summer leaves.

And I sipped my coffee and closed my eyes
and smelled the storm.

Full forty minutes I hunkered down
until the storm rolled away
towards Skipton and the Dales.
Then, smiling, I strode into the rain soaked summer
and watched the steam rise from the tarmac
as hailstones melted in a road-side pail.

Down Memory Lane

A walk from the Author's home around the villages of Pendle in East Lancashire.

A long walk but a good one for winter when the fields are soggy as much of it is on lanes and bridleways.

Nice and varied, hills, fields, lanes and the canal, with an optional detour into Barnoldswick with its interesting little alley ways, independent shops and cafes.

11 miles – allow 5 hours plus however long you spend in those shops and cafes!

Parking - I walked from my home, so you would need to park near the Trawden Arms in Trawden BB8 8RU – a good place to eat on your return.

After a week of heavy rain and unpleasant journeys on the motorways in the wet and dark, I was going a bit stir crazy, so when the sun shone on Sunday morning, I got the house tidy and the washing in and made my sandwiches and customary flask of milky coffee at record speed. 'Should have left it', I can hear some of you saying, but I like walking back in and not having to set to!

As I set off from home, the day was so clear I could see Ingleborough far in the distance from the top of the village. Seeing the table top flatness against the skyline brings back so many good memories of walks in the Dales over the past few years. Dropping down into the centre of the village by the Trawden Arms and turning right up Rock Lane, I had a little peek into the sparkly Christmas displays of the gift shop and saw lots of things I would like but don't need! Opposite was a gift of nature anyway and these are always free. But this one was a little confusing. A cherry blossom tree in bloom, like the one I saw in Langcliffe 2 weeks ago. What is going on? Nature is as confused about the seasons as Parliament seems to be about Brexit! At the top of the hill, I took a left at a bend in the road, this old track leads to the top of Winewall, and as the track ends and you bear left down the steep road, there's my old house on the right, 29 Winewall Lane and I can almost hear my teenagers thundering down the stairs as I shout "tea's ready". Ah – fond memories from years ago! Looking across to Pendle on my left, cloud floated across its flanks from half way up so the familiar ridge was hidden from view, but the views across to Colne with the Town Hall clock and the Church were wonderful and familiar – these were the views from my lounge window for 10 years!

At the bottom of Winewall I turned right onto the main road for about 20 yards and then joined the old tram tracks off to the right, this is a shortcut up to Standroyd Road which leads you up to Keighley Road. Crossing Keighley Road, I followed the roundabout across to the Morris Dancers pub (one of the first pubs I ever went in – ah those memories again!) and then I took a right up Venables Avenue and walked up past Park High School remembering all the years I dropped my kids off at school there. Right – enough of memories, I'm supposed to be living in the moment here! Past the school and left onto Castle Road and the views of Foulridge Upper and Lower Reservoirs and the hills of the Yorkshire Dales opened up. What a glorious place I live in. As the road dips there's a lane on the right leading down to the reservoirs and I followed this, stopping to watch a large flock of Canada Geese sunning themselves on the banks of the very full reservoir. Nice to see it so full after it has been almost empty since July! As I watched the geese, 2 late arrivals were honking their way across the sky and they glided in, landing right in the middle of the group. After crossing the lane which bisects the reservoir, I followed a yellow arrow on my left, climbing over a stile into a very wet field and heading towards Broach Flat farm. Through a kissing gate, boots slithering on the mud I followed the left field edge and inched my way over very slippy duck boards. 45 degrees right now and I was at Foulridge Primary school, all quiet on a Saturday. "What lucky children," I thought, "playing out in these grounds with these amazing views up to Noyna Rocks." They probably don't give it a thought – I know I didn't at age 7 when I was lucky enough to attend Gisburn School.

Following the school driveway down to the main road I turned right and crossed the road after 20 metres or so, looking out for the footpath on the left that skirts Foulridge Lower Reservoir. The sun was shining brightly now and it was off with my hat and gloves and time for a drink of coffee on a well positioned bench.

In contrast to the noisy Canada Geese at the top reservoir, here 2 doves landed silently on the tree right next to my bench. All quiet now for a couple of minutes and then the sound of the pad pad of a runner's feet as he ran past me, his panting breath disturbing the doves who flew off, their wings beating in unison.

Never mind, many miles to go, so I needed to press on. At the boat club I left the reservoir and crossed the little tarmacked lane onto the farm track opposite, there's a yellow footpath sign on the entrance. As I passed old farmhouses, a robin hopped on a moss-topped wall, sun sparkled through bare branches and water rushed and gurgled past twisted tree trunks and ivy covered roots. Ditches that for so long had been dry, were now alive with bubbling, babbling water gushing into a hidden tunnel under the lane.

Past Holly Bush farm and the track ended without any apparent footpath. A gate on the right led into a field and a chestnut pony with a white blaze approached me. "Hello" I said, "Is there a footpath in your field?" But the pony was not amused and ears pressed back, he blew his nostrils and turned tail, flinging mud up in his wake.

'Oh well', I thought, 'I'll consult my map.' However, when I extracted this from my day sack, I found I had brought 'Hedben Bridge and the South Pennines' which wasn't much use when I was near Colne! That'll teach me to put my glasses on instead of thinking I recognise the picture on the front of the map!

Gut instinct told me this field was where I should be and that I should be heading leftish! Sure enough leftish it was and there was a little gate with a welcome yellow arrow. Straight up this field and I was at Whitemoor Riding Stables where for many years I sat and watched Katie trot round the indoor arena, (on a horse naturally!). Now another horse stood in my way, a very big one with feet the size of dinner plates. "You're not on the path!" bellowed the woman who owns the stables, "And watch that fence, it's electric!" 'Oh great,' I thought, 'either get trampled or get electrocuted!' "Just walk past him, he's fine," she said. That's 18 hands of 'fine' to you and me. So if you do this walk make sure you stay in the field and don't go through a gate onto a little lane like I did!

Moving swiftly through the yard (!) I turned left onto the road for about 100 metres and then onto the Gisburn track. It's a tough little climb here but I left a much younger guy way behind me as I marched on to Weets House Farm where the views of the Ribble Valley and the Longridge fells were laid out in all their splendor. On the way, several alpacas grazed in a field and a baby one was sporting a blue coat – super cute! At the gate just past the farmhouse, I turned right onto the Pendle Way and now I was on the moors proper, but it's a good track so no getting lost here. The wind was icy though, blowing right up the Ribble

Valley, so hat and gloves back on.

I love Weets Hill, the sky was blue and the profile of the trig point set against the horizon made it look like a little white chimney puffing smoke across the moors! Time for lunch now, so I settled down behind a wall off to the right and realised that I was looking 8 miles across to my usual picnic spot on the top of Boulsworth Hill!

As I was munching my ham and tomato sandwich, 2 teenage boys cycled towards me grumbling good-naturedly about how many bogs they'd got stuck in, how wet they were and how one of them had just cut his leg on his pedal. "Sounds horrendous, your bike ride," I laughed. "No, it's great fun", they said, "We're coming up on Christmas day, come rain or shine!" I'll stick to my walking I think!

An icy wind blew me all the way down Folly Lane into Barnoldswick and here I had a choice. At the main road, I could turn right and walk about a mile to the road down to Salterforth on the left from where I would pick up the canal-side path back to Foulridge village. Or – I could go left into Barnoldswick and look for tea and cakes. Tea and cakes won, thereby adding 2 miles to my walk and to add insult to injury, there wasn't a gluten free cake to be had anywhere in Barnoldswick, oh dear. My exact words were not 'oh dear' but modesty forbids me from typing them! I walked through the town centre and turned right on the main road to Earby where I contented myself with a large chocolate bar from the filling station.

Just before the village of Salterforth – half a mile or so, I turned right down a snicket onto the tow path and then followed the canal as it meandered under stone bridges, past brightly coloured barges moored for the winter. The tow path was busy with cyclists and bounding cockapoos and their walkers and many smiles and greetings were exchanged as I strode along with my walking poles and gaitors and muddy boots, I looked like I was dressed for the Alps and they must have been wondering where on earth I'd been.
I stopped at Café Cargo, by now desperate for cake but no – even here, there was not a gluten free offering in sight other than a bought-in and decidedly uninspiring finger of fruit cake. Somebody in Pendle needs to open a gluten free café!!

Up through the village to the main road and back to the school, where I retraced my steps over the fields and past the reservoir, the sun now low in a dove grey sky. The Canada geese floated on the silken surface, feathers lit by the pink glow of the approaching dusk. The outlines of the houses and trees on Castle

row were dark against the sunset. I stood for a long while, knees aching a bit from long miles and two still to go, but thankful for this beautiful landscape on my doorstep and for my wonderful Dad who taught me to appreciate the freedom of walking. Back past the pub, back down the tram-tracks, back up the hill where I used to live, back along the track to Trawden, back to my lovely cottage and a hot bath.

What a day, what memories I'd recalled and what lovely new memories I'd made.

Ticking all the boxes

Buckden Pike, Starbotton Fell and the River Wharfe in the Yorkshire Dales.

A high level walk, mostly on good paths. Make sure it's a clear day and your phone is charged as you could go the whole walk without seeing a soul!

Distance 7 miles

Allow 3.5 to 4 hours.

Park in front of Buckden Inn, Buckden Village BD23 4DA

This walk ticks all the boxes for me. A steep pull from a sleepy village, a trig all to myself, a 360 degree view of nothing but high hills, a long descent through a hidden valley and a pub at the bottom!

A bit of a grey murky start had me thinking I may not see much on the tops, but there was some blue trying to break through way ahead on the horizon, so I tried to keep positive. I'd had a hard couple of weeks and was feeling the stress.

There was a biting northerly wind and the temperature had plunged overnight as the forecasters had advised; it was registering only 3 degrees as I parked the car.

Buckden is a tiny village on the east bank of the river Wharfe and I'd briefly visited in the Spring when I walked back along the Dales Way after dropping down from Old Cote Moor. However, memories of Buckden go way back to my early twenties as one of the first big jobs we secured in our furniture making business was making the pine bedroom furniture for the Buck Inn. As I parked up in front of the pub I wondered if the bedroom furniture was still going strong 35 years on! Left out of the back of the car-park is a clear footpath which takes you past Rakes Wood and gradually climbs the valley side. The views

across the valley to Kirk Gill Moor and the surrounding fells are wide and wonderful and apart from a couple walking a few hundred yards in front of me, I had the views all to myself.

I was soon up to the metal gate where you branch right for Buckden Pike and here my fellow walkers and I parted company, as they walked on following the Pennine Journey trail. The path was a little confusing here as the description said continue on the bridleway but there was no obvious bridleway! There was a sort of path straight up by the wall and a very vague path going off 45 degrees left. As the directions said "go through several open gateways in dry stone walls" I decided to go left as there were lots more walls in that direction! I did check my map here and realised that the one I had with me was an OS Landranger map and not my OS Explorer one that shows you where the walls are, oh dear!

It was soon obvious that I was on the right path though as I did go through several gaps in walls and there were lots of boot prints to follow, (always a confidence boost!) which eventually led me to a surfaced route. Here the gradient pulled at the calf muscles and so I stopped for a breather and remembered to turn around and look at the view. Oh my, all of a sudden I was high enough for the familiar outlines of

Pen-y-ghent and Ingleborough to break the grey skyline beyond Potts Moor and Plover Hill. The beauty of it never fails to take me by surprise.

With all my layers on, I was getting warm now so the hat and the gloves were off though the wind was biting as I pressed on up the stepped path. "Who on earth dragged these flags and stones into place?" I thought, as I silently thanked them.

As a family fairly skipped down the path, I stood breathing hard and wondering why on earth I hadn't gone back to walking at a much earlier age! But I was soon up the last steep incline and onto the top and the trig was in view. I slid a triangular stone into a little gap near the top and said to my long lost loving Dad "There you are Dad, another one we've climbed together."

And then the sun came out.

 Heading along the ridge, a flagstone path leads towards the War Memorial on the top of Starbotton Fell. Part way along I found a sheltered little spot behind a wall and enjoyed my simple lunch, just me and the weather and the hills; perfect.

The war memorial commemorates the lives of

5 Polish crew-members who were killed on an RAF training flight on 30th January 1942. Of the 6 man crew, 4 died instantly when the plane plowed through a stone wall in blizzard conditions. A fifth was seriously injured. Jozef Fusniak, the 6th member, despite having a broken leg, managed to construct a shelter for his injured crewmate and then followed fox tracks in the snow down to the little village of Cray, but it took a rescue team 2 days to find the wreckage and in the meantime, the injured wireless operator had died. Jozef (a rear gunner) returned to flying and was shot down just 5 months later in Germany; he spent the rest of the war in a prisoner of war camp. In the 1970s he returned to Starbotton Fell and built the memorial to his crew-mates. What must he have felt returning to that spot? I stood, in awe of the courage of all the men and women who died so that I might be free to walk these fells.

Jozef passed away peacefully in July 2017, for further details of his story follow this link http://www.buckdenpike.co.uk/mainstory.html

A signpost and the odd blue topped post showed me the way down to the little village of Starbotton, a two mile gradual descent through a valley where I looked across to stone walls crossing the valley sides like patchwork squares. "Who built those walls?" I asked the sheep, but they just nibbled and stared and didn't seem to care.

Down and down, with a short stop for a hot drink from my new pink flask!

The sun fully out now in a blue blue sky and the sparkling river snaking below. It was a lovely but seemingly long descent and the old knees were complaining at the last half mile or so on a lane where the stones rolled under my boots with each step.

But at the bottom, joy of joys, the Fox and Hounds pub and half a cider, sitting outside in the sun. Then turning left for a hundred yards, I took a right, down a little path which took me across the River Wharfe where I picked up the Dales Way back towards Buckden. Kicking the leaves and empty conker shells, I walked past woolly bullocks nuzzling each others heads and then I stood for ages looking up at Firth wood, where the spiky green spruce pierced the skyline behind the rusts and yellows of the rounded oaks. Although not as vibrant as the colours I'd seen in New England just two short weeks ago, to me this small wood, climbing the sides of the valley, was every bit as beautiful.

This side of the valley was in the shade and away from the sun, the icy wind was blowing hard from the North and so I was zipping up everything as far as it would go and wishing I'd brought my furry hat with the ear-flaps instead of my faithful little beanie! But soon I was striding into Buckden and following the sign to West Winds tearooms, tucked away behind the pub, where the very kind owner let me have a pot of tea and a piece of gluten free Victoria sponge even though I was 20p short! With a roaring fire and a good selection of food, this is a little café to remember on winter walks.

Boots off back at the car, poles stowed in the boot, I drove along the tiny road to Conistone, the golden late afternoon sun slicing through the trees on my right, thinking about my walk and feeling so much sunnier myself than I had on my drive up there!

Bacon, Boots and Books!

Choose a fine day for this medium length walk above Settle and across Langliffe Common towards Malham tarn. There are long stretches where there's no mobile signal, so be sure that mist or low cloud are not expected.

Distance - 11 miles

Allow 4.5 to 5 hours

Park at Langcliffe opposite the church just off the B6479, 2 miles from Settle. BD24 9NF

When I was seven years old, we lived for about 4 months in an old miner's cottage at Arcow just outside Settle, whilst we renovated an old schoolhouse near Gisburn. I have fond memories of Saturday morning trips into Settle in my Mum's green A35, called Niffy nine-ten on account of its number plate being NFY 910. Parking on the market square, we would buy the weeks groceries at various little shops (no big supermarkets in the mid sixties) and then have lunch in Ye Old Naked Man café.

Travelling up to Langcliffe yesterday, I decided to treat myself to a bacon butty in said café before I strode up into the hills. The café dates back to 1663 and was originally a pub. Local legend says that a naked man was found buried there and that it was once home to an undertakers, but, whatever the history is, I was happy to find that the food was still yummy and the service still friendly.

Driving on to Langcliffe, I parked up in the village car park next to the little old school. Driving along the B6479, you would not know that behind the cottages on the road side, there's a beautiful little village; old cottages nestling round a village green, a Jacobean Hall where Isaac Newton was a regular visitor. In fact he is said to have gained his inspiration for his theory of gravity in the hall's orchard.

Boots on and poles in hand (actually I forgot them and had to come back for them when I got half way up the lane and wondered why it seemed such hard work!) I walked past the pretty church and on up the road that leads to Malham. It was a steep start to a walk and I was soon unzipping my jacket and taking my hat off! About half a mile up the road, there's a sign for the Pennine Bridleway and as the road veered to the left I took the bridleway straight on.

The bridleway weaves its way over moorland, past an old deserted barn and there's a signpost to Victoria Cave if you fancy a little detour, but I'd been late setting off due to my bacon butty stop, so I pressed on. Ingleborough was dark and brooding far off to my left but the sun was trying hard to break through the gauzy cloud above me.

It was very windy the higher I climbed and I realised as I rounded the back of Langcliffe Scar, that I was going to be battling the wind for the next few miles. However, there was a real treat in store for me as I turned east; Pen-y-ghent was in full sunlight and her craggy profile set against the surrounding fells was stunning. I knew that there would be tens, possibly hundreds of people walking up to the summit and I was glad that I was all alone with not even a sheep for company!

Passing by a wood, I stopped to listen to the wind in the fir trees. The sound was powerful and exhilarating like the big choral moments in Handel's Messiah.

Wow, with the wind whipping round my face and the wide skies and the hills rolling on for miles, it really was a moment to remember.

A long solitary stretch now and I did wonder several times if I'd missed my footpath off to the right. There are shake holes and disused mine-shafts up on these fells, so you have to stay on the well defined paths. Along the way, I passed strange patterns of limestone boulders that looked like jigsaw pieces and thought what a great place to bring children and let their imagination run wild.
The weather was looking grey ahead and misty over the fells and there were spots of rain in the wind, but I was fine, after an hour or so, there was the friendly signpost pointing the way to Stockdale Lane phew!

Turning right over Grizedales, I walked by highland cattle, who looked up at me from their chewing and I thought how wonderfully warm their furry coats looked. It was raining now but there were breaks in the clouds ahead and my Gortex was doing its job well. Sure enough, after twenty minutes, the rain cleared and the sun shone as I reached the next wooden signpost and turned right under Kirky Fell and Rye Loaf Hill.

Time for lunch now and hot flask coffee. There's really nothing quite like finding a stone that's just the right size for you and your rucksack and settling down in a sheltered spot with a stream gurgling away in the bottom of the valley and long long views. To sit in silence, thinking of nothing other than the wonder of it all. This is what I walk for, the feeling of being completely at one with nature, completely responsible for myself, completely in awe of the universe doing its thing so beautifully no matter how much mankind tries to destroy it.

Ah well, time was travelling on as it does and I was aware of that change in light that happens around 2.30pm on a winter afternoon and a shift in temperature that signals the move towards dusk. Holding my flat hand to the sun, I counted the fingers between the sun and the horizon – one hour til sunset for each finger, so I reckoned I had 2.5 hours left to get back to the car. Plenty of time.

Striding down the valley side towards Stockdale Lane, the path was slippy due to the short shower, so I was glad of my poles, but I made good time to Stockdale Farm, which must be the tidiest farm I have ever seen. The silage bails are beautifully stacked, the yards are clean, the farm buildings immaculate, it always impresses me.

Past the farm and onto the tarmacked lane now and eventually right at the T junction to walk the mile or so downhill into Settle, then through the tiny lanes of jumbled cottages at the top of the town, keeping to the Pennine Bridleway signs and then up and over the fields for the last mile and a half to Langcliffe.

Dropping down into Langcliffe and my first conversation with a human being! A very nice man called Dave who had been a caving instructor all his life and who now has a boat which he often moors in Carsaig Bay on the Isle of Mull. As this is where my daughter Amy lives, we were soon remarking what a small world it is!

As I entered the village I noticed that there was a book sale sign on the church entrance so I went to investigate. The big old church door was unlocked and the lights came on automatically as I went in. I was soon lost in the cookbooks and the walking books and every genre of fiction you could imagine, then click, the lights all went out and I couldn't see a thing. I was wandering around feeling my way past stacks of books and around pews finding the door and wondering why the lights wouldn't come back on even though I'd opened

and closed the door! In the end my eyes grew accustomed to the dark and I managed to find my rucksack and poles and put my £4 in the metal honesty box and pick up my 4 books and find my way out. Laughing to myself, I wandered back through the village to the car, stopping to photograph a winter cherry tree in full pink blossom.

There was the car and so ended my Bacon, Boots and Books adventure. Face glowing and legs aching in the best possible way, I turned towards home and another working week.

Good enough to do it again!

A lovely circular walk that takes in all the best that the Dales have to offer, starting in the pretty little village of Arncliffe.

About 9 miles

Allow 4 hours

Park in front of the Falcon Inn, Arncliffe   BD23 5QE

Note – There are long stretches with no phone signal and most if it really is away from all civilisation, so if you're not an experienced walker, probably best to walk with at least one other person.

I first did this walk on a day where the weather forecast said rain expected at 2.30pm, however, it arrived at noon, so I spent most of the walk trudging through heavy rain, head down. Four days later, as I sat at my desk in the office at home, there was a power cut and I had no email, no mobile, no house phone etc., so after an hour, doing what I could, I gave in to the message the Universe was sending me and packed my rucksack!

Parking up at Arncliffe, I booted up and set off past couples eating pub lunches on the tables and benches outside the Falcon Inn. It was warm and sunny and felt just exactly how a Spring day should feel!

As I walked along the lane to the right of the Falcon, the craggy grey escarpments so typical of this part of the Dales, rose up towards the blue skies, whilst, at my feet, the lush green of new grass was dotted with the bright yellows of dandelions and celandines. Turning right through the gate signposted Malham 6.5 miles, I was soon climbing out of the valley. This steep little climb had me puffing and panting as I was carrying extra weight in my back pack. I was trying out new summer walking boots, so I'd packed my old ones just in case – I didn't want to be contenting with blisters a good few miles into my walk.
Turning to take a breather, I marveled as I

always do at the glory of the Dales. Stone cottages huddled around a village green, dry stone walls ran up and down the valley sides, a stream sparked below and hills stretched for miles in every direction. Only ten minutes into my walk and already the sounds were purely of nature; a bee buzzing, birds rejoicing and the stream gurgling far below. With a smile on my face, I turned back to the climb.

Through a gate and up, following the valley side, I could see the flat limestone tops of Highfold in the distance and I knew that on the other side, lay Malham tarn and over the next ridge, Settle. Just a few short weeks ago, I'd been looking back from the far side of Malham tarn to where I was now walking.

The path followed the valley side for a couple of miles, passing stone escarpments like sentries standing to attention and when I looked carefully, I could see all sorts of natural sculptures. In the middle of all the sentries was the face of a smiling woman – honest!

Eventually, the path winds left away from the valley and passes through Dew Bottoms under Great Clowder and Parsons Pulpit. Limestone outcrops are ever present, weird and wonderfully shaped like the pieces of a giant's chess set, tossed in anger when the game was lost. Up and over a wall-stile and I was really out on my own now, just me and the moors in the middle of God's county. Not a sound but my heart-beat going 'Da Dum, Da Dum' which brought on a lovey little reverie about Patrick Swayze and the dance-training scene in Dirty Dancing, (fellas – you may not quite get this!).

Rounding the base of a small incline on the left of the path, I could see trees ahead. 'Aha,' I thought, 'Civilisation.' Trees usually being a sign of a farm or smallholding. But I had been fooled. As I approached, I could see that no-one had lived here for at least 50 years. The porch leaned dangerously, the roofs have slipped their slates, the barns were empty. The yard, between the farmhouse, the cottage and the barn, which once would have been cobbled, was a mass of nettles, the windows were boarded and the doors were padlocked. I settled myself on an old cornerstone to eat my lunch, wondering how many farmworkers had eaten their lunch (of baggins, as they used to call it,) in the same spot.

Happy and relaxed, I strode on along the old rutted track, imagining times gone by and farm children, running out to greet their dad as the farm cart rumbled home from the market in Settle.

Soon the track winds left to a gate through which you can see trees and this time they are

not fooling you! Here is Middle House Farm, aptly named, as this is about the middle point of the walk.

I stopped at the gate and had a good look ahead of me. I was looking for a five-barred gate straight ahead, about a hundred yards beyond and across the farm lane. Beyond that about 45 degrees across a field there is a tall stile next to a gate, that's where I was heading. Looking at the field beyond the tall stile I could make out 3 vague paths. Because I'd walked this walk 4 days previously and met the farmer's son which was very lucky (!) I knew I needed to take the left path, but once in the field, this is difficult to see. From the higher vantage point of the gate I was leaning on, I could see the path and I knew that it lines up with a point at the far side of the field where a dry stone wall running left to right, is joined by another straight wall coming over a small hill. I fixed that image in my mind and set off down the slope and over a stile to the farm track. Through the said gate and over said high stile (but there is a gate next to it) and towards the point where the walls join. (Do not rise up the hill on your left.) It took me about 20 mins to reach the far wall, where I picked up a clear wide path and turned left onto it.

This lovely path slowly climbs and eventually meets a wall where you go through a gate and see the path continuing like a green ribbon along the back side of Great Chowder. Across the valley is the hulk of Hawswick Clowder - according to the English dictionary, Clowder means a group of cats but I couldn't quite see the connection!

Far and away the moors rolled beyond Conistone Moor to the North Yorkshire Moors under a hazy sky – perfect. Time for a coffee and a cream egg!

After half a mile or so, the path follows the remains of a wall on your right and as the wall ends you go through a gate Here, there seems to be a path going off at a right angle alongside a wall. Don't turn right, go straight on and the path you need begins to emerge again and after 5 minutes walking, it starts to drop down. Soon I was passing a sign to Arncliffe Cote and picking my way carefully down a steep little path. A good test for the new boots which are intended for the West Highland Way in a few weeks.

The rest of the walk was down and down, looking across to the swell of Hawswick Common on the other side of Littondale and beyond to the higher ridge of Langcliffe – a climb for another day. Four days ago, this had been a wet and dreary slog, now it was just wonderful. Huge lung-fulls of fresh air, birds chorusing, the late afternoon sun turning everything gold and warming my shoulders. The quiet was so quiet it was loud and I felt huge and yet knew I was just a dot on the landscape. Nature is a healer and I so needed to heal. It was only 8 weeks since my Mum had died after 5 awful years battling dementia and grief seemed like a big hole I kept falling into. But up in the hills, even when a few tears fell, the wind soon dried them and even the sheep seemed to be saying 'there, there' as they looked at me and bleated. It's hard to feel sad for long in the midst of such beauty. Eventually, I saw the green caravans of Littondale Caravan and Leisure park below me and soon I was in the farmyard of Arncliffe Cote Farm, where an exuberant black Labrador insisting on giving me his chewed up old slipper, several times! Across to my right, a rabbit was making its way carefully across the beck, hopping leisurely from stone to stone – amazing.

I walked down the farm lane to the road, between trees laden with pink blossom and past nodding bluebells; spring flowers scenting the evening air. At the road, I turned right for about 150 yards and just past the entrance to Littondale Caravan park I turned left onto a single track road which leads down to the river. At the river I took a left before the bridge, picking up the sign for Arncliffe 1.5 miles. This seemed a long 1.5 miles, probably because I took a call from my son and ended up missing a gate and walking round 2 large fields several times!   However, it was a lovely end to the walk, watching the sparkling clear water of River Skirfare splash around boulders and meander under the old oaks and horse chestnuts and soon I was walking past the old reading rooms onto the village green and back to the car. A little late to enjoy a cool cider outside the pub unfortunately; the daisies on the green were closing up for the evening and the midges were already nibbling, so the boots and poles went back into the boot and I set off along the valley back towards Grassington and Skipton and home.

A super walk, done twice in the space of 4 days and the new boots were fine!

Wisdom

Dear Reader

I hope you are enjoying this book and finding that it 's one you can simply pick up whenever you need a break from our busy world.

Before you embark on the next section of the book, I 'd like to explain why it is written in the form of letters.

In the preface, you learned that I had crashed and burned for the third time three years ago. On my release from my hospital, my very wise eldest daughter took me to a Buddhist Monastery in the Spring of 2016 for an enforced rest. Whilst there I met, very briefly, someone called Jenny, who quite simply, made me believe I could change.

Over the following two years, I wrote letters to her charting my progress. But I couldn't send them, as I didn't know anything about her, other than her first name.

The letters will explain to you, dear reader, my journey from an overwhelmed and exhausted workaholic, to someone who is kind to herself and starting to feel contented. I hope you find some wisdom within the lines and that you too, are on your own path to contentment.

Much love, Wendy

2nd May 2016

Dear Jenny

There is mist on the hillside and dew on the grass, the crows are "caw cawing" and hundreds of small birds are singing. The gong has sounded for morning meditation and I am writing. At last, I am writing.

Through the window I see the tops of tall pines swaying gently against a backdrop of scudding clouds. The only sound is the rain pattering on the puddles. I made you a promise and I have kept it; I have returned to the monastery to start writing.

Firstly, dear Jenny, let me say thank you for giving me the courage to start this journey. For in sharing your experiences and trusting me enough to tell me 'your story', you showed me change is possible, at any stage, at any age. I do not know if our paths will ever cross again, but what I do know is that you came to me at just the right time and even though these letters may never actually reach you, it seems right that I should write them.

I have been searching for ways to find contentment for many years. In my past, dear friends have no doubt tried to show me the way, but it was only in my lowest moment, when I was absolutely spent, that you showed and I finally listened.

I open my laptop and feel my heart soar as the birds sing their morning praises.

Jenny, how did I come to be sitting opposite you that morning, feeling so ill and believing I was a failure? I am one of those people of whom others say, "I don't know how she does it!" I am constantly busy: an irrepressible entrepreneur, a volunteer on several boards, a presenter and speaker, an influencer; as well as being a mother of four, a carer and a wife. It sounds exhausting just reading it doesn't it? Then there's all the other things I try to fit in: walking, reading, time with friends, writing my journal, baking, playing the piano, writing poetry and watching my wonderfully creative children act and sing in bands.
All my life I have felt that I pack as much into a day as most people pack into a week and I always thought that in doing so, I was getting so much more from life than others. How brilliant to be so

industrious, so busy that I couldn't possibly sit still, with all my lists of things still to do and my brain constantly in action.

I enjoy being asked to talk at business dinners, conferences and seminars, even if it means travelling half the length of the country for no more than expenses. I'm wanted, I'm needed - my expertise, my experience. They tell me I'm inspiring, wow! And everywhere I go, there are new, interesting people to meet, to follow up and have phone calls or meetings with, exploring the possibility of working together. Adding more and more people to my contact lists and never having time to do anything useful with any of them. I am continually trying to find more and new ways to search for fulfillment, to try and achieve success.

All this, I managed to tell you over one cup of tea.

"Aah, success", you said, with a knowing look in your eye, "But whose definition of success is that?"

I don't know what drew me to you Jenny, there were around sixty people in the refectory that morning; some deep in thought, some chatting to others at the long tables, some sitting in the quiet area. I was recovering from a four-day emergency admission into hospital, where nothing had been found despite X-rays, Ultrasound and MRI scans. I was suffering from acute stomach and back pain, only sleeping if I took Dihydrocodeine plus Paracetomal at four-hourly intervals and here I was, deposited at the monastery by my eldest daughter, after a scathing lecture which included phrases such as "When are you finally going to do something for you?" and "We don't give a fuck about the money, we want years with you and at this rate you are going to kill yourself."

I had been in no state to argue as she rammed things into my lovely new Osprey rucksack, which was supposed to be accompanying both myself and her across 96 miles of Western Scotland on the West Highland Way. I had been so looking forward to walking this with her again and I was truly disappointed in myself, because I knew that, for the fourth time in the last six years, I had worked myself into the ground.

Through tears, I kept half -heartedly trying to tell her I was too ill to go away. "Rubbish", she responded, "If you need to come home, you can ring Glenn (husband) to come and get you, it's only two and a half hours away, and if you need urgent care, they do have hospitals in Dumfries you know."

So, there I was, standing with my bowl of porridge, feeling like a naïve teenager on a school trip, scared of who I might find because I had been made to stop and take a long hard look at myself; and there you were, smiling.

Sometimes, you get to know someone so quickly, it feels like you must have been very close in another lifetime. That's how I felt about you before I'd even finished my breakfast. You understood me after about three sentences. You'd had your own wake up call about five years before and had managed to stop for six glorious months and take time out to review your life, which resulted in you making your own journey to contentment.

Jenny, one of the first things you and I talked about was time and I've been thinking about it since. Like all the best things in life, time doesn't actually cost anything; the problem is that most of us believe we do not have enough of it. But the fact is that there are 1440 minutes in each day and each one of us can choose what we will do with those minutes.

But can we choose really? People have responsibilities and bills to pay: we have to work, look after children or elderly parents, or we ourselves might be ill. The minutes, hours and days go past in a blur. I get that, I really do, I have spent all my life believing I have no time to do the things I really want to do, precisely because I have followed the path of career, business, marriage, children and eventually dependent parents, which is exactly why I was sitting opposite you, Jenny, on that fateful day.

When my daughter dropped me off, the day before I met you, I stood there, my new aqua green rucksack by my feet, watching her yellow Citroen disappear down the drive and I was very scared. Me, who hopped on and off planes to Europe with abandon, presented confidently to 200+ people, negotiated unheard of deals with tax officials on behalf of clients; stood there fighting back tears in front of some big white statue thing of a Buddha in the middle of what looked like a building site.

What the hell was I doing here? Why couldn't I stop the tears that were threatening yet again. "Hello there," said a bald lady in burgundy robes with a serene smile, "Are you OK?", "Not really" I said, "I think I'm just going to cry for the next five days". "If that's what you want to do," she replied, "then that's fine."

I took refuge in my simple room: a bed, a chair, a single wardrobe, looking over a courtyard garden. I made up the bed and sat on it. I cried again, my stomach hurt; deep sharp pains that had me doubled over. "Get a grip," I said to myself.

I put my walking boots on, walked slowly down to the river and stood watching the water flow, just watching how it flowed around the boulders and rocks. When faced with an obstacle, it altered its course slightly, but kept on flowing. Could I do that? Alter my course slightly, find my flow? It all seemed too much like hard work.

Why did my daughter bring me here? Buddhism and monks and chanting, living in the moment? It was fine for her, with her yoga and her folk singing, her single status, her life of friends and travel and hope.

But me, 56, past my prime, my best work behind me, the wonderful years of raising children gone, a marriage being rebuilt after a horrendous situation a year ago; now facing my own mortality every day as I watched my mother slip further and further into dementia. 'Life's a bitch and then you die'. What was I doing in this hotchpotch of a place? For that's what it looked like to me, flags draped on trees, a half built garden, mismatched buildings and a red and gold temple, in the middle of forests and hills. Mad, it all seemed slightly mad!

That first day, Jenny, the day before I met you, I felt panicked all day. Somehow, I got through lunch, slept most of the afternoon, ate a simple meal in the dining room at 6pm, just keeping myself to myself, not trusting myself to talk to anyone, tears threatening all the time.

In the evening, I ventured into the communal lounge in the main house, the original building that had been here in 1967, when two Tibetan brothers, Dr. Akong Tulku Rinpoche and Chogyam Trungpa Rinpoche, founded the first Western Tibetan Buddhist centre in these beautiful rolling hills of Southern Scotland.
Adjoining the old fashioned, comfortable lounge was a treasure trove of a library; shelves bursting with books of every genre, from faith to chick flick fiction. I sipped a mug of warming tea and chose an interesting novel and then spent a long time picking up and discarding all sorts of poetry, autobiographical and spiritual offerings. Finally, my hand settled on a slim book entitled 'Living in the Moment' which appeared to be a short biography of someone who used to visit the monastery. 'Best pick

that' I thought, as living in the moment seemed to be the 'in thing'. Books in hand, I snuggled down into the corner of a vast sofa and prepared to read.

But actually Jenny I didn't read anything. I spent the next two hours listening to and then joining in some lively conversation about the speed of life in the 21st century, which led of course to me explaining a little about why I was there. Except, I don't do 'a little'. I gush, I spill, I cover everyone in the minutiae of my life, whether they want to hear it or not. Looking back Jenny, I was out of control, totally stressed out, hyped up, overwrought and they, poor things, good naturedly let me rant.

I couldn't get to sleep that night. My room was next to the main door of the building, which banged whenever someone came in or out. Plus, I was next to the girl's dorm and there was a lot of talking and laughing going on. Added to the mix was the pain beneath my ribs, which felt like my liver was about to explode, so there wasn't much sleep happening. At about 2am, I decided that first thing in the morning I would call Glenn to come and take me home, I was really struggling and couldn't believe I had been stupid enough to let Laura bring me here. I sat up and wrapping myself in my fleece, picked up the slim volume and started to read. I was amazed to find that after a few pages of biography, the book was filled with the most beautiful poetry.

I don't think I told you in our short time together, but my childhood and teens included taking every piano, ballet and poetry exam in existence; once we said we wanted to try something we weren't allowed to give up! However, in doing so, I developed an enduring love of both writing and reading poetry. Scanning the first few lines of a poem, I know immediately if I will like the feel and shape of it and one in particular felt right as soon as I read the first two lines.

The poem I was drawn to was called 'Gnosis' and as I read it, it genuinely seemed to be talking directly to me. When I read the last four lines, I felt as though a thunderbolt hit me, much as I did the first time I met the love of my life. Something profound happened. I read it over and over, maybe seven or eight times. After reading it, I settled down feeling safe and calm for the first time in a very long time. The author of the poem was Christina Worsley, who for a short time, was a nun at the monastery. When she left, she remained a practicing Buddhist and frequent visitor to the monastery. Sadly, Tina, as she was known, passed away in 2009 in her fifties. She left a legacy of beauty and wisdom in her collections of poems and songs and I will be forever grateful that my hand settled on one of those collections when I was so in need.

With the kind permission of Lama Yeshi Rinpoche, here is the poem that finally made me realise that looking for the next client, contract, project or board position would not lead me to happiness.

GNOSIS

Please don't try to find me,
If you look – I won't be there,
I'm not in any textbook,
Sitting in an empty chair
Beside a spider's spinning wheel,
Or creeping on the stair.
If you look – you'll never find me,
So don't search – and I'll be there.

Please don't try to find me.
I'm an animal that's rare.
You can't trap me in your silver nets,
Or track me to my lair.
The nearer that you get to me
The more I'll move away.
Don't look for chains to bind me –
When you break them, then I'll stay.

Please don't try to find me
With a map or crystal ball.
For searchlight beams I'm much too large,
For microscopes – too small.
I'm not through the darkened window
Where the glass is smashed and gone,
But the moment that you look away
My light will surely come.

Never try to find me.
I would threaten you to stay.
You would struggle if I held you –
I don't want to win that way.
The more you look, the less you see –
Perceive your own despair –
When you decide you'll look no more
Then I'll be everywhere.

Christina Worsley

During the night, reading the poem, I eventually admitted that I was searching for happiness in the wrong places. But working out how to even start breaking the habits of a lifetime seemed overwhelming.

When I met you, over my porridge Jenny, I was about as low as anyone could go.
But, over two breakfasts, one vegetarian lunch and one bowl of soup, your smile, your compassion and your absolute belief that I could break those habits, changed my life. At that first breakfast, you persuaded me not to call home, to give the monastery a chance, to just take a breather, just sleep and read and sit a while and it sounded so good, I decided to stay.

Isn't it strange, we only spent about four hours together, but it changed my life.

Jenny, you will have heard the expression many times, "You can lead a horse to water………" and I will be forever grateful to my daughter Laura for leading me to my enforced sabbatical, but I will always wonder; if I hadn't read that poem? If I hadn't met you? Would I have 'drunk' the water?

Much love, Wendy

4th May 2016

Dear Jenny

Before I return home, I must write you another letter from this haven, this place of safety and solitude where you gave me so much in such a short space of time.

I felt a bit lost when you left in the taxi, we'd been to morning prayers together and although meditation was new to me, I had managed to absorb the beauty of the temple, the gentleness of the place and I'd been able to slow if not stop my thoughts altogether. With a big hug and a final promise that I would start to write, I waved you off.

The weather was kind that day and I was feeling strong enough to tackle a short walk. Packing a note book and novel into my lovely rucksack, along with my waterproofs, (because, after all it was Scotland!) I set off towards the tiny hamlet of Eskdalemuir. The sun was warm, the rolling forested hills rose up from the valley and the light danced on the river. I have always appreciate beautiful scenery and often stop when I am walking to drink in the view, but on this walk, I stopped and looked right in front of me. Close up. A dewdrop on a leaf showed me an upside down world. A little branch became a Pooh stick bobbing away under a stone bridge. I sat on every bench, I looked at blades of grass, I smelled the pines, I tried to 'live in the moment'. Every time a thought outside of the moment came along, I visualised putting it into a box and posting it back to my office where it could wait until I was well enough to deal with it. My phone and email said I was on holiday, my mind would have to accept it too.

It was a revelation. I can remember every detail of that walk. The conversation I had with a guy doing his garden, the taste of the coffee in the café, the smell of wood smoke as I crossed a farm yard. Life is in the detail and you can't see the detail at 100 miles an hour.

I only walked about 4 miles and slowly at that, but as I walked beside the river looking up at the hills these words came to me.

I had a little wander and I had a little ponder
Just ambling along by the river 'neath the hill,
I had no destination, no planned or written goal
I just set off walking and I waited for my soul –

to find me.

Then it kind of hit me
As I stood beneath the hill,
How can it ever find me
Unless I stand quite still?

I needed to find myself again Jenny and I needed to really slow down to do so. Stopping altogether couldn't happen because of commitments I had to adhere to, but if I really slowed down, cut back my working hours, could my soul find me again? That short walk was the start of my journey Jenny and a good start at that.

* * * * * * * * * * * *

Things come in three's right? Well, you were number one.

After a sleep, because the short walk had floored me, followed by the customary soup at 6pm, I went to Chenrezig Prayers and lost myself in the beauty of it all. By now, I was falling in love with the monastery. I didn't even notice there was building work going on at the front and the gardens were half finished. All I saw were smiles everywhere, all I heard was birdsong from morning to night, the lounge was comfy, the café was cosy and quiet and my bedroom was simple and safe. There were wise and wonderful people working and living there who were happy to listen and never judge.

Something about the place, the fact that I was away from reality, encouraged me to have wonderful open conversations and I had many of these with other guests and people who were living there for extended periods. There seemed to be an unspoken agreement that here was a place you could just be you, your CV was irrelevant and wow did that feel good.

Good thing number two was a monk who had had been in the lounge that first evening. Leaving a wealthy corporate lifestyle in the 80's, he'd travelled widely and after much soul searching, became a Buddhist and eventually, a monk. After listening to me that first evening in the lounge, he had uploaded a pen drive with information, talks, films and video clips that he felt would help me personally, but also be useful in my work. He sought me out the day after you left and told me his story and about the work he now undertakes around the UK helping totally stressed out people to change their lives. He knew I would need a lot of time and support to change and here was a toolkit I could dip in and out of at any time. This love and kindness oozed out of everyone I came across at the monastery.

Good thing number three arose from a conversation I had with a guy who was visiting from the Samye Ling Centre for World Peace and Health on Holy Isle. Over soup one evening, he talked to me about the wisdom of Lama Yeshi and suggested I arranged an interview with him before I left. "OK" I thought, "this sounds good, this feels right."

But before I get to that, I must tell you about how I laughed, truly and freely for the first time in years, during the same 'soup' conversation. I was telling above 'guy' about how stressed I have been for years and how the magic of the monastery was already calming me down, after only a few days. I talked about how I had no patience, how sarcastic and short-tempered I was, especially with Glenn. I also talked about how I'd been thinking back to when I was young and optimistic and felt free, wearing my 70's long skirts and beaded necklaces. "Well", said wise guy, "I'd love to be a fly on the wall when you get home. You'll glide through the door in your hippy skirt, with a loving smile on your face and instead of shouting at Glenn for watching the TV when the floor needs hoovering, you'll walk over and give him a big kiss and say , "How's your day been, my lovely husband?" and Glenn will sit there in a daze thinking 'Who is this woman? Where is my wife? Bring back the bitch in the business suit!'. Well, you would think, we'd all had several drinks. We started laughing and could not stop. It was that infectious laughing you do when you're 14 and with your best mates. It was fantastic. Even now, every time I think of it, I giggle.

But, back to the impending appointment with Lama Yeshi.

Now Jenny, I am not well known for focusing, I usually have several plates spinning at once and I am always too excited by the next new opportunity; so focusing on what exactly was the key issue I wanted to talk to the Lama about in my allotted 10 minutes was something I thought would be difficult for me. Plus, knowing that here was a man whose advice is regularly sought by world leaders, I felt somewhat in awe.

But in Chenrezig prayers that evening, listening to the soothing chanting, it came to me. It was clear to me that in order to even contemplate the journey I was about to embark on, I needed to resolve something that was eating away at me. Could a short conversation with one man really sort out years of hurt and anger?

It could and it did.

Much love, Wendy

5th June 2016

Dear Jenny

Once again I am enjoying the beauty of Samye Ling and I write as the mud dries on my boots, which have kept my feet dry on the hills high above Moffat. I have walked for five hours today and seen not a soul. I have crawled up a hillside so steep I dared not stand up in case I fell off backwards! I have jumped for joy as I discovered a path when I finally reached the top. I have talked to my Dad who is present on every hilltop and in every mountain stream and at Chenrezig prayers this evening, I have thanked the Universe for this truly brilliant day.

And now I continue my story in this letter to you, my dear and inspirational friend.

I don't need to tell you or indeed anyone, about the detail of my conversation with the Lama and I know you will respect that. There was a lovely guy at the monastery who was also struggling with something and he saw the Lama after me. On a long walk, we helped each other reflect on the advice we had been given and marvelled that one wise and compassionate man could so quickly have understood our suffering and enabled us to find a way to let go of it.

For that is truly how I felt, like I had unclenched my fist and let the wind blow the hurt and anger away, like the dandelion seeds you blow on as a child to tell the time.

I will never forget the Lama's words and to recall them gives me strength when I feel that this long journey I am embarking on is too hard. For, as you will know Jenny, amidst the reality of life, it is very hard to make the smallest of shifts.

As my health recovered and Spring burst forth on every hedgerow and tree, the reality of making ends meet once again took precedence. I needed to earn and that meant planning, selling and delivering. Whilst I was ill, Glenn worked seven days a week to cover the bills and he was looking very tired. I needed to step up again and quickly.
Holding on to the decisions I made in the simplicity of the monastery was very difficult against the reality of rebuilding my earnings in a country in crisis over the impending EU referendum. With

151

business confidence at a low, companies reigning in spending on training, difficult tenants not paying rent, teenage kids with their own traumas and Mum wandering the corridors of a nursing home looking for her memories, my life was complicated and exhausting.

But somehow, for a few minutes a day, hold on to them I did. I knew I could not once again fall back into the old routine and more importantly, I knew I didn't want to.

I needed to find ways to simplify the hell out of my life and some hard decisions had to be made about work and personal commitments.

Why do people let life get so complicated and so busy Jenny? Why do we keep saying yes? Is it so we feel valued, important? I think it was in my case.

Many women, myself included, start a business because they want to make a difference. That difference can include a better work-life balance for themselves: but often they want to help, nurture, inspire or support. For many, it is not the 'be all and end all' to make a lot of money, build a large business, achieve a multi million turnover. This is why so many women are involved in social enterprises and the Third Sector.

In my case, 18 years ago, I wanted to help small business owners to understand the basics of business growth. I wanted to ensure that they never had to live through the hell my first husband and I found ourselves in when we literally came within 24 hours of losing our home, business and lifestyle. With three young children under five, it was one of the most distressing periods of my life and all because we didn't understand how to manage a business well.

Incredibly, we did manage to keep our business going, paying off every penny we owed. It took us seven years, and in those years we learnt the things every business owner should know; business strategy, planning, finance, marketing and people management. So when my first husband and I went our separate ways in our mid-thirties and I eventually left the company we had built, I knew I could teach business management well and I knew I wanted to teach small business owners.

So at age 38, with a four month old baby, a new husband, my three children from my first marriage aged

13, 12 and 9 all living with us in an old terraced house which needed completely renovating, I thought it was a good time as any to start my business venture!

Did a little bit of me want to prove to husband number one that I could build my own business? Probably. But as the years went by, the driving force for me was always 'helping'. Especially helping small business owners who were in a financial mess and needed to raise finance or do deals with the tax man and suppliers, because in essence they hadn't managed their business growth well.   I loved the urgency of situations like this, the thrill of persuading a VAT officer to delay a court case to give me time to start managing a business out of a loss into a profit. I loved the trust business owners placed in me, often allowing me to totally manage their finances for months or even years. It was stressful work getting involved in the very fabric of a business turnaround and I often had several projects on the go at once, but I had worked under pressure for years as we turned our own business around and on reflection, I guess I had become an adrenalin junkie.

So the years passed Jenny and as the children grew I was able to work longer hours, further afield, taking contracts on in Europe and travelling regularly to London and Austria. I established and ran a successful women's business network because there wasn't one in the vicinity and I was invited onto my first board. I became defined by my work and lost if I wasn't busy.

A standing joke in our family is 'Wendy on holiday'. Day one, Wendy vows to relax and sunbathe, Day two, Wendy finishes her first book, Day three, Wendy is going stir crazy and has to plan a trip. The trip to the French Village Cow festival has to be the most desperate trip of all but it was the only one I could find on a Tuesday in June in the middle of the Vendee! Bottom line; I am incapable of relaxing. In fact in my mind relaxing is the same as 'wasting time' and that makes me feel guilty.

Where did this ridiculous behaviour come from? Well, my childhood.
As far back as I can remember, my days have been filled with industrious occupation. My mum didn't go out to work until I was at secondary school but I rarely saw her sit down. She would be up ladders painting the gutters, or decorating, or making curtains. She held coffee mornings weekly, went to the Townswomen's Guild, sewed all her clothes and ours, baked twice a week and arranged superb dinner parties for my Dad's clients. Dad was the Sales Director of a decent sized company and was often away on business. When he was at home, he was gardening, growing our veg and fruit, standing as a Liberal

candidate, renovating our houses and volunteering at Newspapers for the Blind. My siblings and I went to piano lessons, elocution, singing lessons, ballet and tap, from the age of four and of course we had to practice piano every day and learn our poems and do our homework and set the table and wash up and help in the garden and wash the car; I'm sure you get the picture. The whole of my childhood and teens continued in this vein and I clearly recall being at my boyfriend's house at 5pm after finishing my Saturday job when I was 16 and my Dad yelling at me down the phone to get home as I hadn't done the ironing. I got a clout for saying "For God's sake" as I walked through the door and then I got grounded for a week just for good measure. Ah well, the joys of being a teenager.

Seriously though, this is where my 'learned behaviour' of never relaxing comes from.

I couldn't play out until I had done my homework, my piano practice and my jobs. Lights had to be switched off when you left a room, cushions had to be plumped up when you rose from the sofa, doors has to be closed to keep the heat in. You measured the water going in to the kettle, woe betide you if you ate a piece of newly baked cake if some of last week's cake was still left. We used to call the old cake 'qualifying cake'. It's all still there going round in my head.
It drives Glenn nuts that I can't sit down until the kitchen is tidy, the floor hoovered, the washing folded and put away, the curtains closed 'just so' and the lamps lit.

Thankfully and with the help of Glenn, I have somehow managed to raise four wonderful children who work hard but do not have an aversion to relaxing! They have really balanced lives, amazing hobbies, are creative, have full social lives and have travelled far and wide.

My eldest as you will recall Jenny, was the one who brought me to the monastery and in so doing, led me to you. She also persuaded me to take up walking when I was 54, something I hadn't done seriously since I was a teenager when I walked extensively in the Lake District with my best friend's family who were members of the Preston Mountaineering Club. Walking is in all probability what has kept me sane over the past few very difficult years of supporting my Mum who so very sadly has dementia. Getting out and up into the hills has kept my soul alive – just.

On reflection then, I understand why I cannot relax. Can I change this learned behaviour? We will see. My original question near the start of this letter was "Why do women especially, keep saying yes and just let themselves get busier and busier?" I have thought long and hard about this and for me I think it is as follows.

My businesses have always remained small. I kept them small deliberately because I was also a Mum of four and I wanted the agility and flexibility that a small business gives. I operated with a handful of part time staff and a network of associates. It's a good model, but looked at against traditional measures of turnover, number of employees, profit i.e. when you measure the GVA (Gross Value Added), it's nowhere. As a result, although my expertise has saved many companies over the years and helped to grow dozens more, you will never see my businesses featured in a regional business magazine or winning a business award. This lack of recognition can feel unfair and I know this is why I was flattered to be invited to join local, then regional and finally a national board; it felt like recognition of that expertise.

I think wanting to be recognised and seen as a success by the local business community is part of what has driven me to work crazy hours, accept offers to present at conferences far and wide, join four boards as a Non Executive Director and eventually to crash and burn four months ago. And as you so rightly said when we first met "Success? – whose measure of success is that?"

Much love, Wendy

3rd August 16

Dear Jenny

I am at the monastery and again it is raining. August and today has felt more like April, but even in the rain it is beautiful here. The misty hills seem soft and gentle and the place feels like sanctuary.

I am fully recovered from my illness now Jenny and desperately trying to stick to my goal of walking for several hours on Saturday or Sunday plus half an hour each evening. I know I am being more sensible about work and have been known to shut my laptop and head for the hills in the mid-afternoon, now that's a break through!

I have set aside three days every six weeks to come to the monastery and I am determined nothing will get in the way. Things are hectic at home and I am not sleeping well, so it is so important that I come to this place where I do unwind and find myself again.

I don't think I told you just when I first started to rediscover myself Jenny, it was about half way through those first five days at the monastery.

You will recall I said that I felt like a teenager when Laura drove away and left me with my rucksack. As the week went on and my make up got left off and I stopped talking about work and I just walked and reflected, I realised that the time I started to discover 'me' was aged 16, during the two years I spent at college.

It was my decision to leave an all girls grammar school and go to college, the first decision I had ever really been allowed to make and as I recall, one that didn't go down too well in view of the fact that my mum and dad had moved counties so I could go to the grammar school. But somehow, they let me go and even bought me a moped to get from the village to college. At 16, I finally felt a little 'cool' as I sped along the bypass (well at 30mph) in my flares, my Levi corduroy jacket and my suede ankle boots and when I turned up at college, although I didn't know anyone, it felt good to be me.
I loved college. I loved the fact that you were treated like an adult and it was your own responsibility to turn up for lectures. In addition to 'A' levels, I took a contemporary dance certificate in my lunch hours,

I was in a great local drama society and undertook several lead roles, I was in college productions, I was Rag Queen. I scraped through my 'A' levels mainly because, instead of studying, I spent hours at my boyfriend's farm. I got engaged on my 18th birthday, which made me something of an icon amongst the female students!

When I started college, I wanted to be either a countryside ranger or a journalist. I'd starting writing journals and poetry at age 11 and I loved writing as much as I loved being in the country side and walking. I was going out with a farmer's son and thought I would one day be a farmer's wife and I loved the prospect. At the start of college I thought I would go off to University and take Geography and Biology, by the end I was already helping my fiancé to build a business making wooden kitchen accessories. I was young, I was in love, I was buying a house and getting married and my parents were horrified. Don't get me wrong, they liked my fiancé, he was hard working and from a lovely family, but they wanted me to go to University, to see the world before I settled down. Looking back, how wise they were, at the time I thought they were old fashioned and trying to control me.

I was married at just 19 and we worked all hours building the business. The dance and drama fell by the wayside as work took over. The business made very little money for the first five years and I had to be the breadwinner. I took a job in insurance straight from college, was managing three branch offices by the age of 23 and working evening and weekends doing our business accounts and even working on the factory floor if we had some big orders in. We had 15 or so employees by the time we were in our mid twenties and looking back we had to grow up so fast, we never really got to be young and carefree. Between 25 and 30 I had 3 children, we moved house twice and also bought our mill premises. The business grew to almost a million turnover and the children and I saw less and less of my husband. He worked seven days a week and at least four evenings until 11pm. I worked school hours and ran the home, our social lives, taxied the kids here there and everywhere, plus did the decorating and the garden. It was draining and looking back at my journals (I've written 35 of them so far) from those years in photographs, I look tired and drawn.

It was during that time that I wrote the poem opposite after watching a documentary about old people looking back over their lives.

You see Jenny, I was in a marriage where work always came first but I didn't question this because I was the product of an upbringing where I was constantly told "If you work hard you can achieve anything". Looking back, the only time I followed my heart and truly felt free was at college.

On about day four of that first week at the monastery, I realised that, from the age of 18, I hadn't followed my dreams, I followed my husband's. Over the years, instead of becoming a writer or working in nature, I became the Finance Director of a manufacturing company. My journals and the many poems I had written throughout that period must have been the real me longing to 'get out'.

Even when I set up my own business it was around business finance and although I did return to drama and take my teaching diploma, I didn't use it, as it wasn't anywhere near as lucrative.

So why oh why, did I end up a workaholic, chasing other people's versions of success, when all those years earlier, I had written a poem that demonstrated so clearly that I didn't want to end up like Robert Bray or his wife!

How could I change what I had become? It's easy to promise to change when you are surrounded by peace and wisdom, with time to think and reflect, but could I really break habits of a lifetime, still earn a living and also be true to the real me?

Much love, Wendy

Lost Moments

His voice, like his suit, was respectfully grey.
"The last will and testament of one Robert Bray."
As he started to speak, her own voice rose instead,
"Too late for lost moments" she stood up and said.

And as they all turned, she gave way to her rage,
The hopeless frustration of all the lost days
came at last to the surface – and spilled down her face,
Tears for those moments now lost without trace.
"Work comes first." she spat out the words
that all through her life it seemed she had heard,
"Well, work came first and now here is death
and all I have left is this destitute wealth."

"You can keep all your papers and all they contain,
I'd give everything in them and start over again
and this time I'd take every moment God sent
and each second, each minute, would be truly well spent."

"For what is a life filled with nothing but working?
Shirking the pleasures that money can't buy?
We used to say next week or next month or next year –
Well now here's forever and nobody's here."

She picked up her bag, moved away from the table
"Don't get up" she said, "I'm really quite able
to cope on my own, to get on with my life,
I've done nothing else, I was Robert Bray's wife."

4th December 2016

Dear Jenny

Even in the stark simplicity of winter this place is still beautiful. The drive over the forested uplands looking over the hills at the northern end of Eskdale has me grinning from ear to ear, while I deftly avoid the potholes, which seem to get deeper with every passing month. I walked those same hills in August and ate raspberries off the hedgerows, now their promise of fruit is hidden deep within their dark winter branches. But at the monastery, the birds still sing, the river still rushes around the boulders and the magic prevails.

The gardens are almost completed at the front of reception now, with a fine arched wooden bridge leading to the river walk and a water feature bubbling away soothingly. I still like to go the old way past the Tibetan tea-rooms and the shop, down the little side path – the way I first walked to the river all those months ago when I was so poorly.

Maybe you've visited too and seen the progress?

Anyway, where were we? Ah yes – can I change?

I did feel different when I came home and Glenn noticed a change, I certainly wasn't as short with everyone: he didn't want the 'bitch in the business suit' back!

Work-wise, it would have been easy to slip back into those long hours, trying to impress people, giving my time on all those boards.

At first, that wasn't an even an option, I was still not well and a third visit to the GP finally confirmed that I had shingles which took me a couple of months to get over. I was in pain for weeks and exhausted, so I worked short days and only four days a week and I was determined to keep it that way.
During those weeks, I watched some of the contents of the pen drive given to me by the kindly monk and dipped my toe into the teachings of many wise spiritualists, scientists and Buddhists. One of these,

Greg Braden says "Ask not what this world can give to you but what you can do for this new emerging world." It has enabled me to start planning my journey from overworked and overwhelmed to a place where I will still be making a difference, but not in a way that was exhausting me.

I decided to spend two hours every Sunday morning watching some of the content, which was fascinating. Scientists and historians weaving together the most ancient of wisdoms with the most recent discoveries, challenging Darwin's theories based on survival of the fittest and instead talking about how our planet has evolved through cooperation not competition. I was intrigued by a practice called Heartmath and wanted to learn more about our energy fields and our heart intelligence.

I started walking regularly and came across a big old boulder at the foot of the hill some two miles from our home. This became my 'thinking' stone. Fortified by a flask of coffee and a chocolate bar, I spent a lot of time considering the work I had done over the years. What had I enjoyed most and where was my expertise needed?

I couldn't start a brand new career based on dreams of long ago, I needed to earn. With a mortgage and Mum's care bills rising, I didn't have that option.

But I did need a new business model. One that earned me enough money in fewer hours, one that I enjoyed and importantly, one that helped other overworked business owners. That was very important to me. I asked myself some fundamental questions. How much did I need to earn in a year and how many hours did I have available to earn it? Then, I turned my usual method of planning on its head and worked out my next 12 months based on how many holidays I wanted. How many trips to Samye Ling, how many days a week I wanted to walk. These things – not work, I prioritised. That left 190 days per year to earn what I needed.

Next was the decision on how to earn it. My current model was based on me, selling and project managing, paying other people to deliver. But I didn't enjoy project managing, I loved advising and mentoring the client. Problem was, I couldn't deliver the service that was currently our main earner, my expertise lay elsewhere. Could I change what we delivered and stay true to the company mission and vision? Where and how could I use my expertise in business analysis, strategy and finance and how would I get in front of the client again?

Then, there was the stuff on the pen drive. Dipping into that had led me to Heartmath, the resilience building and stress reduction coaching method I longed to bring into my work. I needed to change my product offering, pay for and attend a Heartmath course and earn enough to make up for the period from March to June, where I had been ill and not done any selling. Against a backdrop of small businesses being cautious in the wake of Brexit, it was a tough ask.

I also reflected upon how much I'd been doing that I didn't get paid for. Did it bring me any other benefits? Did I get referrals or did it raise my profile? If the answer was 'no' then it had to go. Within a fortnight, I gave up two regional steering group positions and when a national Non Exec board role came up for a three-year renewal in July, I also gave that up. That was a tough one, the role had given me a lot of credibility and raised my profile in the business world, but it involved monthly trips to London and around the UK. Everyone else around that board table was salaried, but each time I took two days out to attend, my earnings stopped. The position had to go. "It's on my CV", I thought "and no one can take that away". Being a Non Exec over the years had given me new contacts and experience and I maintain it is a good way to build your credibility as you build your business, but too many times we do too much for free and I was a huge culprit.

How could I work towards this new model? It was a huge change and I knew I needed to approach it using small steps.

I decided that I would work to a 1:3 formula. What that meant was each week I would complete one fairly large task and each day complete three small ones. All of which must take me nearer to my goal of doing more of the things I love doing at work. It was simple and more importantly, it was do-able.

I had to explain to my trainers that I was changing the direction of the business and that their work would gradually phase out – (that was a large task). Then I had a good long look at what was on my doorstep, where was there a gap in provision that I could fill? What had I developed in the past that had been successful that I could resurrect?

And do you know what happened Jenny? When I started to concentrate on what I loved, what I felt passionate about, the doors started opening. An old work colleague invited me on a free sales coaching course, it felt right, so I went. That led me to developing a new course with her and eventually into a great new working partnership. An ex-employer asked me if I wanted to earn commission finding clients for a local business support programme they were delivering. "No" I said, but I will bring you female business owners for the commission as long as I can deliver my own business support package to them for a day rate of £xxx. You can have the sign ups and outputs and I get a route to clients.

I had needed to simplify the hell out of my business and working life and I felt like I was succeeding.

Now I needed to tackle earning enough money.

Over the years I have seen that a lot of women undervalue their skills. They may have worked in a corporate world where their hourly rate to a client was £x hour plus, but once they set up on their own, they think they are only worth a third of that! For many years, I had fallen into this trap and various (male) mentors along the way had told me I was way too cheap. I decided to increase my prices by 50% overnight for all new consultancy clients. I did this and no –one even questioned it.

At my new hourly rate, I could deliver client facing work three days a week, deliver one training event every couple of months and make enough money.

I also got tough re referrals. For years, I had referred clients to trusted trainers and consultants thinking that they would return the favour – but they rarely did.
So, the next time a client needed a referral to an associate, I negotiated a decent referral fee before I introduced them to the client.

It's great to connect people in business, but when you've done all the business development and brought the client on board, you cannot "gift' that client away.

By the end of August, I was really enjoying work and all the walking was keeping me healthy and sun tanned. Jenny – was I cured? Had I re-programmed? Could it really be so simple?

Much love, Wendy

5th December 2016

Dear Jenny

Oh – how all the good intentions slip and slide when you're back in the thick of it. When the nights are drawing in and the house is a mess because your husband has decided to convert the loft and your kids have problems and your Mum's nursing home is not looking after her properly and your tenant has wrecked your flat and the contract you thought was a good deal, takes twice as many hours to deliver as you thought it would.

The days I promised to set aside for my learning, the walking, the trips to Samye Ling, all lost their priority status and as they did so, my sleepless night returned, my right shoulder ached, my writing stopped.

I wasn't ill or back where I had been in the Spring. I was still enjoying my work and just about meeting my target income, but all the 'me ' time had disappeared.

It is difficult to motivate yourself to walk when the evenings are dark and weekends are often wet, especially when you are a lone walker. My husband will walk if we are on holiday and very occasionally on a weekend, but his idea of walking is very different to mine. I am moved by views and get excited about buds on trees and the sun glinting on water. I stop and sigh and take photos and sit and sip my flask coffee. He doesn't get it, he just wants to walk. He's lovely and funny and gives the best cuddles, he just doesn't want to go on walks.

So it's very easy in the dark evenings to just cuddle up instead!

September to December is a busy time for business trainers and there was a lot of interest in the courses I had developed for Women in Business. I designed them, sold them, organised them and delivered them. I found new consultancy clients, re-wrote much of the website, re-designed my marketing material, did all my admin and accounts work and wrote daily tweets and weekly blogs. I was often working until 8pm.

On top of this, as a family, we were now struggling to pay my Mum's nursing home fees as we had moved her into a smaller, family-run care home, costing £700 per month more. To cover the additional fees and not eat into her capital, we needed to convert a property we had bought, from a disused store to a flat and the management of that was talking up hours of my time.

The more tired you get, the easier it is to slip into the old routine. You forget the 1:3 plan, you forget to plan your diary, you accept coaching sessions and consultancy half days all over your week. You forget that it's easier to work your contact book than go to new networks, you just don't think straight.

Then, before you know it, it's the run up to Christmas, the most stressful time of year for many women and it starts way back in October, as soon as the Halloween costumes are off the shelves.

To add to this crazy mix, Glenn is shattered and unhappy at work. In the summer his whole section at work transferred onto continental shifts, so he now works 12 hour shifts, three days, four nights then vice versa, with only one day in between, then every four weeks he gets eight days off. He is like a sleep-walker all the time except for the eight days off.

Then on his days off, he is helping my son David, convert the property we have bought from a disused shop into a flat, to create more rental income to cover Mum's nursing fees.

Unbelievably, we are not falling apart and I know that some of what I have learnt since March is working. I do not nag as much as I did, I do not criticise like I used to. Occasionally, I even do romantic things like leave little notes all over the house for when he gets in and I'm out. One on the TV remote, one on a bottle of beer in the fridge, one on the mirror in the bathroom. Worth a medal I think after 20 years of marriage!

I'm not where I expected to be though Jenny, I thought I would be much further along on my journey and I need to get back on track.

But I am coping with stress far better than I had ever done and I know that this is down to the Heartmath techniques I have learned so yes, I did find a way to attend the course.

I managed to negotiate a monthly payment plan with Heartmath and started the course in July. This involved Skype sessions with a trainer, a lot of reading and a residential course, followed by more Skype sessions for you to 'practice' being a coach on your trainer!

When I met the other delegates on the course, I automatically did what I have always done in life – judged them by their outward appearance. I know I have learned this from my mother, who, even in the grips of dementia, says things like "Fancy letting yourself get to that size," or "She looks a miserable thing."

I am not proud of admitting that this is exactly what I did when I met my 17 class mates and listened to their short intros. "He looks like a know-it –all'" "She looks sloppy."etc. and I immediately picked out about three people who I thought were 'like me' and who I would target.

I will also admit that after the two hour introductory session on the first evening, I thought I had been duped. A month's earnings just to learn how to breath? Oh no, what had I done?

But how wrong could I be?

I learned so much in those four days, four days that were almost as life changing as the monastery.

I learned that if you deliberately use your physiology and thoughts to channel appreciation into every breath and if you compound your own appreciation by sharing the experience with others, it totally changes the way you feel about people and situations.

In some ways, what I learned was the simplest and most automatic thing we do from the moment we are born, breathing; in other ways, it was the most profound learning I have ever received.

When I came back I had learned how to prepare for, deal with and recover from challenging and stressful situations in the most simple and natural way and people started to notice. I had also had a hypnotherapy session, which I was very sceptical about. However, on the last day of the course, I finally succumbed. During the session I was simply asked the question "Who are you?"

This was very revealing. For, every time I was asked "Who are you?" I answered "I'm a mother" or "I'm a wife" or I'm a daughter" or "I'm a business-woman". Finally after many gently probing questions, I felt a huge opening up around my heart, an incredible outpouring of feeling and without me seeming to think the words, my voice said "I am Wendy and I am good." The strangest thing then happened. I knew that in that moment I felt like I did when I was at college, when I was 16, when I was 'me'.

I walked back into the final two hours of the course and knew I felt like I had at 16 and in a college lecture, I was so aware, so focussed, so free. I felt like I'd been viewing the world with a 40 watt light bulb on and now I'd replaced it with a 100 watt light bulb. You might think I have lost it Jenny, but I know that I'd found it.

What about work and Heartmath? Well, now, in addition to concentrating on what I could deliver myself directly to clients, I was licenced to deliver basic Heartmath techniques and exercises and I could build these into workshops and coaching, helping other stressed people to learn about resilience and balance.

Much love, Wendy

24th March 2017

Dear Jenny

Too much time has elapsed since I sat in my simple room at Samye Ling and felt the urge to write. It never arises at home and even here, this time, has only surfaced after a long walk through the woods near Langholm and a stunning drive back through the hills.

It's a year Jenny, since I met you and I wonder where and how you are; I hope you are well and happy.

I am moving in the right direction finally, but only after veering madly off course in the New Year and applying for a CEO position because I was seduced by that word I mentioned way back in my June letter to you. Recognition.

A job I had my eye on for years came up and I knew I could do it. But as soon as I read the job spec in early December I knew deep down that I didn't want the hours, the responsibility, the constant representation, the travel. So I didn't apply. But then, four people whom I really respect and admire, individually contacted me and said 'You are going to apply aren't you? – you'd be superb in that role'.

Ego stepped in and said "Ah – recognition at last!" So for ten weeks I then focused nearly all my attention of my application, preparing for three separate interviews, having conversations with my peers across the UK, reading economic strategies and Brexit opinions. All the time my head was saying "The salary, the position" and my heart was saying "No time to write, no closing your laptop and setting off on a walk mid afternoon just because the sun is shining, no chance of synchronising your work days with Glenn's, no extra couple of hours sleep if you've had a bad night."

The whole thing excited me but also terrified me. So when they rang me and said 'Sorry you didn't get it" I was a little disappointed but mostly I was relieved. I wanted the job for all the wrong reasons.

This whole story must tell you Jenny, just how much I need to get back on track, back to doing what feels right, back to being 'me'.
This four days at Samye Ling, it has taken me a lot longer to start to relax, I am so far away from the

realisation that came to me last Spring.

I must stop searching. I need to be still and listen to my inner voice. It is so very difficult not to fall into that fatal trap of ego.

How can I combine the way I want to be with the things I need to do?

Buddhism teachings are all about waking up to this moment, seeing this for what it is. How can I cut through the confusion of everything I have experienced, thought, felt and seen and 'awaken'? Maybe if I stayed here for six weeks, I could start to understand? Maybe it's like when you let your eyes go out of focus, so you can see a 3D picture?

What I do know is that the more I allow myself to move towards the things that feel right, like working with women in business, like walking, like writing, the happier I am and the happier the people around me are. So maybe that's a good place to start.

It's difficult to try and describe the early morning at Samye Ling to someone who has not stayed here. You'll know what I mean Jenny – the gradualness of it; waking to nothing but birdsong, the gentleness of this place. Even on holiday there is often hustle and bustle and bedroom doors slamming and other people's showers running. But here, all is calm and unhurried and even those who rise very early for 6am prayers are quiet and respectful of those needing more sleep.

Breakfast is 7 to 7.45 and the short walk from my bedroom to the dining room is a joy. Hundreds of birds on the feeders and hedgerows, the sun rising over the hill on the far side of the river, the frost sparkling on the curved bridge.

There is friendship in the refectory and you can choose to sit in a silent area or not. Sharing a simple breakfast with some you know and some you don't, is a lovely start to the day. After breakfast you can join morning meditation, but my meditation is a walk along the river, retracing the steps I first took a year ago, when I watched how the water flowed around those boulders.

Today, I think about all the people who have walked by this river over the centuries, for a river is timeless and sustains the body and spirit of thousands over the years.

After my walk, a shower and a visit to Johnstone House to make a cup of tea to bring back to my simple bedroom and sip as I write this and as I do so, I feel calm, lucky to be alive and excited about the walking I will do later in the morning under the blue sky on the green, unchanging hills.

How different to most people's mornings, jerking awake as the alarm sounds, crashing into the violence of the day's news as the laptop, radio or TV is switched on, rushing to shower; then dressing and feeding children and remembering sports kits, or dinner money or reports worked on late into the evening. Grabbing a coffee in a cardboard cup and topping up our caffeine levels. Feeling stressed from the moment we wake, the adrenalin pumping through our veins, damaging our bodies. Running to buses, cars and trains and crawling through lanes of traffic, worrying about start times and deadlines and punishing schedules.

We can choose how we start our days, we can prepare things the night before, we can decide not to look at or read about the world until later in the morning. We can share breakfast, we can say thanks for the new day in whichever way we choose – a walk, a prayer, meditation, a few deep breaths in the garden.

It's hard to re-create the magic of Samye Ling in a busy working life, but it is possible to make small changes that mean a big deal.

Much love, Wendy

18th August 2017

"It is not talking of love, but living in love that is everything"

Dear Jenny

Here I am, sitting in the café at the monastery sipping a rose tea and I've just noticed this quote on the little cardboard tab hanging over the side of my mug. I hope you are living in love Jenny, I certainly am and can honestly say that the more I stick to my promise to 'be me', the more my live is filled with lovely people wanting to help and support me.

It's hard making changes though – real life means needing to earn and after nine months of Glenn struggling with his continental shift pattern, he moved to another job where he could work day shifts again but that meant a 25% pay cut. Through the Spring and early Summer, money worries resulted in many sleepless nights.

I'd invested so much time chasing after a job I really didn't want, that I'd stopped all my business development work, so by May I had very little work. Then a secured consultancy job, due to start in June, was delayed by the client for three months. These things happen all the time in business and you just have to throw yourself into 'selling mode' but it's tough getting out there and presenting a confident front to the world, when you're tired and worried. But get out there I did and that's when the Universe sent me an angel.

Now it's not often that an angel presents itself in the form of a financial adviser, but the Universe sent me an angel and in May, there he was standing right in front of my exhibition stand and I felt immediately that he was sent to help.

Here was a guy who usually deals with people who have millions in property and investments and he simply handed me a card and said 'Let's have a coffee and I'll see how I can help". I hadn't even told him I needed any help!

For the first time ever in my business life, I no longer have help with admin, book-keeping, marketing, follow-up calls…. all those things which must be done alongside delivering work to keep your business tidy and strong.

But, working for yourself, also means you don't have anyone to discuss money with or bounce ideas off.

Now, you would think, that as I am an experienced business mentor, I would recognise the fact that I needed someone to talk to; but like a plumber with a leaky tap, I couldn't see it. In walks Kevin, my angel, who I immediately knew I could trust. Over a coffee, I hit him with everything, the life story, the bank statements, the spread-sheets with monthly monies in and out, the life policies, the pensions.

You're probably thinking, what a clever guy, he knows Wendy is well connected and works with business owners daily, she'll introduce him to clients. You might think he thought I had money, I have a nice car, live in a cottage in a village, have a business etc. I'd have thought like that two years ago, when I was a stressed out, cynical wreck. But now I know better. If someone offers to help and it feels right, then I'm letting them in.

What a great decision, what a lovely, lovely guy. After two hours of him really getting to know Glenn and I, he just took everything away and said "Don't worry, you've made some really good investments re property and rental income and you're in a good position. I'll look at how we can ease your cash-flow and keep your Mum's fees covered. " I actually slept that night.

Three months on, he has sorted everything out, we are in a safer, more lucrative position and he has made a huge difference to mine and Glenn's peace of mind.

He has also introduced me to a superb business group, who meet fortnightly, are all mad as hatters and who support each other in business. I have made new friends, gained new clients and met a wonderful lady who is keeping me on track with my writing. Because, even if you are a coach, you still need a coach.

So, life at home goes on and somehow, against this backdrop of money and work and the sadness I feel when I visit Mum and she struggles to remember who I am, I must be making progress Jenny, because it has taken me far less time to relax into the calmness which descends upon me at this magical place. You will recall, in a previous letter, that it took me a good two to three days to feel inspired to write. This time, I have been here less than a day and the words are flowing.

Each time I visit Samye Ling, it looks a little less like a building site as more of the work on the buildings and gardens is completed. There is now a new parking area beyond the temple and gardens with a series of stepped pools, fed by a Buddha fountain. Plants and bushes, which were newly planted last year, are growing and filling borders and beds with shades of green. The kitchen gardens are filled with vegetables, salads and herbs at this time of year and rabbits hop about under the trees.

Inside, there are no major changes and I'm often given the same room I started to write in almost eighteen months ago. You still have to wander down the corridor to the communal bathroom, but the showers have been modernised a little; you don't have to keep pressing a button and only getting 20 seconds of hot water! What is lovely is that many of the monks and nuns remember me and seem genuinely pleased to see the progress I have made.

The weather doesn't change though, it's raining hard as I write to you! But yesterday, 'ah', what a day yesterday was. Glorious blue skies stretching on forever, warm sun and a cool breeze, perfect was walking, which is just what I did. Up onto the tops above Langholm and over into Tarra valley, which is totally unspoilt. Just one tiny little road with passing places, reminiscent of Mull, where my middle daughter now lives with her partner. Nine glorious miles of me and the rolling hills of Dumfries and Galloway, I only saw two walkers and one cyclist all day. Heaven.
Now this might not be your kind of heaven, but I sincerely hope that you have discovered yours and you glory in it regularly. Walking is the thing that keeps me centred when I am managing work, home, properties, Mum's money and life in general. I do well in the summer months, averaging 20 miles per week, but winter is harder and not spending as much time in nature definitely has an effect on my state of mind.

Walking inspires me to write blogs and poetry. Whereas, in the past, I mainly wrote poetry when I was deeply sad, now I find musings on how I am changing my life for the better, coming to me during long walks. I am sharing some of these on Linked In and Facebook and receiving many positive comments, which further inspires me to write.

I wrote the following two weeks ago when I sat down and ate my lunch way up in the Yorkshire Dales.

Consider

Consider the stream.
It does not worry about whether it is flowing in the right direction,
It just flows.
It welcomes the rain...
Because it renews.
It does not need adornment,
It is complete
and so.......
It sparkles in the sunlight.
It has many voices:
A giggling gurgle, a soothing swirl and the crash and roar of a sudden downpour.
It doesn't ask
It doesn't want
It just is.
Consider the stream
and dare to dream that you too could learn to be
Just be.

20th August 2017

Dear Jenny

Today, I stood by the river in almost the same spot where I stood when I was so ill, all those visits and months ago. After a night of rain, the water was crashing round the boulders, dark navy and deep, with coffee and cream froth and foam and spray. I thought back to the first time I stood there wondering if I could learn to flow around obstacles and keep moving towards my chosen destination.

You told me it was possible and I am beginning to believe it now though it will be a journey as long as that of a river. Meeting you helped me create that bubble of a spring, which is gradually widening into a stream of self-discovery. When I let myself 'flow', incredible people come to the banks of my 'stream' and dip their hands into my life. As the waters of my 'stream' wash over their hands, I learn, I gain confidence and I find new friendships.   When I start to fall into old habits of needing to be seen as successful by the wrong people, chasing recognition, or working with clients who are building a business for the wrong reasons, then the waters become muddy and obstacles, like old leaves and dead branches, get stuck, creating a dam. It's easy to feel like I am starting to drown again when that happens.

I meet so many people who are drowning.

Drowning

At my wits end
No money to spend
Tried everything,
sold everything.

No time to think,
no time to plan.
Snatching at work
wherever I can.

Lost all my confidence
Charging too little
Trying to cope
With a smile that is brittle

Just treading water
Getting so tired
Throw me a line
Just throw me a line………

If I throw you a line
Will you promise to hold
Though the waters be choppy
And scary and cold?

Will you start to believe
Will you find me some time
Will you trust me to lead you
Will you let me be kind?

It will be a long journey
But it's been done before.
Take a breath and start swimming
You'll soon see the shore.

I am sure you will agree Jenny that when you feel like you are drowning there are two things that are key to survival; take some slow deep breaths and stop thrashing about.

Panicking and not breathing will only help you 'drown'.

I was talking to a lady today in the canteen and she said how interesting it was that I've managed to come so far on my journey, by myself. Without therapy or meditation groups or medicine or a coach and so I explained that I hadn't really done any of it by myself.

I couldn't have started without you Jenny. You made me believe I could change.

The monastery gave me the distance and space to stop and think.

The Lama gave me permission to let hurt and anger go.

The Heartmath trainers gave me simple daily techniques to reduce stress.

And when I started working with the right people, they opened doors into rooms full of energy and light.

Most of all, I wouldn't have done any of this or made a single change if my wonderful eldest daughter Laura, had not sworn at me and forcibly deposited me at the monastery with my rucksack and my painkillers.

When you accept that you need to change, it can really help, having someone to help. Someone other than family or friends. Someone to hold you accountable.

I talk a lot about change when I am presenting. Change is the basis of all the work I do with individuals and businesses.

Recently I've talked about change using props so that the audience will remember the stages you need to go through.

I show my audience a pair of earphones and I talk about people I see out walking or running who are listening to music on their i-Pod or phone. They are listening to their favourite music, the type of thing they always listen to. "Take the ear phones off" I say, the first part of change is listening to your surroundings. Listen to the birds, the wind, the brook babbling, the sheep baa-ing. Translated into personal or business change, this means "Be prepared to listen to something new". Be open to new ideas, listen to all your employees, listen to your customers, listen to a new adviser.

Next, I show my audience a pair of binoculars, not any old binoculars, these are the binoculars my Dad used to have slung around his neck on all our hikes up in the Lake District when I was growing up. I tell the audience about all the clients who say to me "I keep looking but I can't see clearly," or "I keep looking but I can't find it." "Stop looking out there" I say. "Turn the bloody binoculars around." "It's not out there, it's in here".

STOP, STAND STILL, LISTEN, LOOK INSIDE YOURSELF. THAT'S WHERE ALL THE ANSWERS ARE.

Next, I show the audience a map and we talk about how dangerous it can be to start out on a walk without a map, plus, you need to be able to read the map and work out where the hills are, where the roads are, where you might have to cross a river. Most important of all, you need to have worked out where you are heading long before you set off. In business I relate this to business planning. For individuals this is about setting goals.

Next are my walking poles. These signify support. Change is difficult, you may need support in the form of experts, systems, tools, possibly investment. Get help, it will keep you on track.

Next up are my walking boots. Once you've got the right equipment and support, taking small careful steps is what's needed. Change is scary. If you take small steps you will still get there, as long as you keep on the path.

Finally, I show my audience my flask of coffee and bar of chocolate, because on any journey you need rewards. You need to know at what point you will get a reward and what that reward will be. If you employ staff and you are taking them on a journey, regular recognition and rewards are paramount. For individuals, it's so important to have someone who says, 'Well done' and recognises that you have reached a point along your journey.

 It's nearly time for supper now Jenny, a simple meal of vegetable soup and then I will enjoy evening prayers.

Much love, Wendy

22nd October 2017

Dear Jenny

I am sitting once more in the café at Samye Ling after a day giving my new walking boots a crash course in Scottish bogs, mud and streams that should be paths, I am exhilarated and ready to write. The birds are pecking at the food on the bird table, the mist is on the hillside and I am writing.

Well Jenny, I didn't get chance to write any more of my last letter because when I wasn't learning, I was sleeping! When I was last at the monastery I joined a course entitled 'Leadership Embodiment' which was led by Amanda Ridings.

I was curious and excited and a little apprehensive. But as happened when I joined the Heartmath course, I met some amazing people and learned new skills to help others.

The course was totally absorbing and because it involved listening to your body and learning to align your core, heart and mind, it was exhausting and emotional.

The course was called Resilient Leadership and so I thought that it would fit really well with my focus on coaching business owners and managers. If you've ever listened to Simon Mayo on Radio 2, you may recognise the three word challenge. You have to sum up your day in three words.
I can sum up my weekend as 'Not as expected.'

On Friday evening we met our course leader, Amanda Ridings and our 14 co-learners and I was soon intrigued. Our course did not seem to be what I had been expecting. We were going to switch off our minds totally and use our bodies' energies to understand presence and empowerment and we weren't going to talk at all as we learned the techniques.

Now Jenny you're probably wondering why I didn't check out there and then and head home down the M6 – I can talk for England! But over the past 18 months, I have learned much about the value of silence and stillness, so I knew the weekend would be good for me.
Our mind has developed over our lifetime and responds to situations and information by rote. It has

built-in responses and reactions and resorts to habits, which are deeply embedded in our consciousness. Amanda referred to our mind as our 'personality'. Our 'self' on the other hand is the truth of who we are.

The practices and techniques, which were beautifully and gently delivered by Amanda, are based on the principles of Aikido and Mindfulness and bring awareness of the body's reaction to stress and pressure. They enable individuals to connect with 'self' and move towards goals or purpose. The founder of the course, Wendy Palmer, has taught many leaders throughout the world, using her techniques, which she developed in the 1960's.

By Saturday evening we were exhausted and Sunday morning we all looked dazed. To 'switch off' your mind and listen to your body and keep centred and keep relaxed and breathe correctly is tiring stuff. But even scratching the surface of this practice was amazing.

I was so pleased that the weekend was not just another Leadership course. Instead, it was another fascinating step on my journey to liberate the real Wendy. The one who writes poetry, the one who walks on the hilltops, as well as the one who uses her skills to help businesses grow and the people in them to flourish.

When you think about it, great leaders are the ones who not only connect with their followers, but truly connect with their own self and purpose, so the course was 100% about leadership.

Since my last letter, I feel I have made two more steps forwards on my journey of change.

The first step involves the Heartmath techniques. I use these daily to keep me focused and calm and I have started to include some of the exercises in my workshops. However, it was only in the summer, that I finally included the 'Heartmath registered coach' qualification on my Linked in profile and on my business website.

Not long after, a lady emailed me to say she was interested in receiving some coaching which I must admit scared me somewhat. Coaching one-to-one was a big responsibility. What if I couldn't explain the science correctly, what if I made things worse for her?
I called my tutor and talked things through with him. "Wendy" he said, you've done all the training,

you've practised on me, you have years of mentoring experience, go do it!"

Why was I doubting myself Jenny, when I spend many hours each week, advising people to believe in themselves and their experience?

I rang the lady and arranged a time for her first session. Three months on she has written me the most amazing testimonial and says I have changed her life. In reality, she has changed mine.

She has made me absolutely sure that my new skills are integral to all the business mentoring and coaching I do. Teaching people to manage stress and anxiety, in a way that fits into the busiest of lives, is amazing. Watching them start to slow down and rediscover what brings them joy, is humbling and it's all thanks to that kindly monk loading a pen drive with information over 18 months ago!

So many people, men and women are presenting a mask to the world of competence, responsibility and fulfillment, but underneath that mask, is a different face. One of exhaustion, unhappiness, and addiction.

People are addicted to stress, to being busy, to being bombarded with noise and information.

People are defining themselves by their work, more and more. At business meetings and networks, people answer "Busy", when I ask them how they are.

'Busy' is not how you are. 'Happy' is how you are, or 'tired' or 'lost'.

Heartmath is enabling me to teach individuals to reduce their stress levels, just five or six practices each day provides a path through the maze of 'busy-ness' and helps them slow down the hamster wheel enough that they can contemplate the scenes of their live and decide which ones to focus on.

More and more I am being drawn to helping others to work on their own resilience and create a life vision that fulfills them and I find my many years of business experience and my recent life experiences have equipped me well for this role.

The second step is profound.

I'm a writer right? Well, here I am writing this book, but if anyone asks me what I do I say, "I am a business consultant working mainly with women in business."

Even though, every morning I practice an Aikido 'wake up affirmation' routine in which I say 3x "I am a writer", I don't think I truly believe it. Even though I have been writing every day since I was 11 years old and I have nearly 40 journals and folders full of poetry and countless blogs, I still don't describe myself as a writer.

Why?

I think it's because of two things.

One – nothing I've written has ever been published.

Two – I don't get paid to write, I get paid to deliver business consultancy and coaching.

Something fundamental inside me says that you are defined by what you get paid for and not by your purpose and I don't think I'm the only person that thinks this.

However, I do recognise that whenever I move towards my purpose, it feels very right. I had lunch with a colleague the other day and mentioned my poetry. We talked at length about it and she asked me why I am not writing and performing regularly. She said when I talked about it I glowed. In fact, she came up with the idea of arranging an evening with Wendy Bowers, where I talk about the journey I am on and perform my poetry. This would be combined with wine and nibbles and networking and money raised from the evening would be used to deliver the inspirational mentoring events I currently deliver in colleges but which some colleges struggle to fund.

I have tested the water re this idea during 2017. I am often asked to speak at business events and usually the presentation I give will include some element of my own business and life journey. Increasingly through 2017, I have found myself speaking about resilience and including some of my own story alongside examples of the Heartmath practice. Sometimes, if it feels right and I know the audience will be receptive to it, I perform the will-reading poem I introduced you to in an earlier letter and the response has been a wonderful surprise to me. Women and men in the audience are visibly moved, many come up to me and say the poem really resonated with them. Women often cry. Some come immediately and ask me if I will be their coach. Some contact me after a couple of months and say the poem has given them the jolt they needed to change their life in some way.

In Parker J Palmer's book 'Let your life speak' he talks about vocation being the point at which your true self and voice meet the needs of the world in a way the world needs to receive them. When I perform poetry, I feel this happening. Something shifts within me and within the atmosphere in the room and I am beginning therefore to wonder if my true vocation is to blend my poetry and maybe that of others, into presentations for business audiences.

Could it be Jenny, that I found Tina Worsley's book and her poem 'Gnosis' to lead me to this very understanding?

Much love, Wendy

13th February 2018

Dear Jenny

I am here at Samye Ling again for a few days, letting the magic of the place and the people soothe my soul again. Instead of rain, which seems to drift over these hills most days, today we have snow. In fact, we have so much snow that I may be here for more than a few days and would that be so bad?

For the first time on this visit, I am back in the room where I wrote my first words to you. The outline of the tall pine trees, their branches weighted with snow, is breath-taking and on the hill opposite, tufts of moorland grass break through the smooth expanses of white snow; it is intensely beautiful. On the ridge of the garden building opposite, a single black crow is studying me intently whilst another sits on the tallest tip of the tallest tree.

Last time I was here in October, I found the Tina Worsley book again, the one with the poem in that spoke to me so profoundly when I was so ill. I'd found the book immediately on my second visit and then, every time since, although I have searched the library, I have never come across it. In October, my hand moved instinctively to a shelf and there it was, the slim white volume entitled 'Living in the Moment'. I held it to my heart, willing my gratitude to cross some time divide and find its way to Tina.

That evening I absorbed the wisdom of her words once more, noting that three poems in particular spoke to me. The next morning, I took the book to reception and asked if they knew how I could contact Tina's family to ask permission to use three of her poems in my work. They remembered Tina and advised me that one of the nuns in the office might be able to help as she had personally known Tina. This beautiful nun, the same one who had accepted my need to cry on my first visit here, listened with interest to my story and my request and said that Tina had been a wonderful woman with a real passion for life and great sense of humour and she thought that Tina would love the fact that her poems meant so much to me. Although she did not think they had any record of Tina's family, she felt sure that Lama Yeshi would consider the request and noting my email, she promised to let me know the outcome. A couple of weeks later the promised email arrived with Lama Yeshi's kind permission to use the poems and conveying his belief that Tina would want her words to be shared wherever they would bring both inspiration and comfort.

So, there I was feeling like I never wanted to let go of Tina's book again, in case I never found it again and then over lunch I found myself sitting next to a lady who was in the kind of state I was in when I first met you. Like the saying goes, 'What goes around, comes around'. This lady was experiencing her first visit to Samye Ling and needed of a little reassurance so, just as you had done with me, I shared my story with her and then I found myself handing over Tina's book. I left after lunch so can only hope she found something in there that spoke to her and helped in some way. Interestingly, I cannot find Tina's book this time around, but I did hear a voice in the library that said to me "you don't need the book anymore, you are writing your own poetry now."

Jenny, my learning journey is continuing. In early November I attended a two- day writer's workshop delivered by Hay House. I discovered Hay House through my interest in Gregg Braden, as they are his publisher. Louise Hay was one of the founders of the self-help movement in the 1970's, long before the West was reminded of the link between mind and body and her subsequent career both writing and publishing is truly inspiring. She died aged 90 on the 30th August 2017 and if you are not aware of her, I urge you to discover her.

Hay House only deliver one writer's workshop per year in the UK and I felt very lucky to be able to attend. Although I've been writing each time I visited the monastery, I haven't been sure what shape my book should take and I certainly didn't know anything about how to approach an agent or submit a book proposal; so when the course popped into my email, I kept going back to it with this question going round in my head. "Am I really a writer and can I make my morning affirmation come true?" I felt that by attending I would maybe find out.

Jenny, it was amazing! Three hundred creative and curious people coming together to learn produces an energy in a room that I have never experienced. Not having attended University, I had never shared lectures with so many people who had a genuine desire to learn the subject. I was like a sponge soaking up every word and every exercise. I met so many incredible people; women with crazy clothes and jangly bangles, businessmen who'd given up millions and lived on the streets in South America, people who regularly spoke to angels or fairies or whatever else they believed in. I truly felt like a writer sitting in that room and it helped me to see that I was making good progress with my book. Plus, I came away with invaluable knowledge from authors, editors and publishers and the opportunity to enter a competition for a book deal. Since the course, I have felt enabled to talk more freely about my writing and poetry and I have been posting fortnightly blogs on Linked In that receive a lot of views and good comments. I have also started to regularly perform my poetry when I present to business groups and it makes me feel so alive.

So here I am again at the monastery and when I walked into the dining room on my first evening, I felt immediately very close to you: I wondered if you were in the room. I scanned all the tables and no, you weren't there, but I wonder Jenny, have you visited Samye Ling very recently?

I do hope you are loving life Jenny and that your vocation is bringing you joy every day.

For the first time, Jenny, I am at the monastery with my daughter Laura, the one who brought me here all those months ago. We are going to do some walking together but also spend time apart. Laura has seen me change over the past two years and has perhaps noticed this more than my youngest daughter who still lives at home. She has seen me becoming stronger, more accepting of other people's choices and mainly she has seen me becoming happier.

I know that I have learned to listen more; the habit of cutting into other's conversation has been a hard habit to break and I don't always manage it, but I really try to be conscious of it.

I know that my body is stronger because of all the walking I do.

I have learned to still my mind when it is racing or full of critical thoughts.

I appreciate the things I have so much more and rarely yearn for the things that I used to feel signified success.

I feel incredibly lucky that I can choose to do the work that I love and can balance this with 'me' time.

I am telling the world that I am a writer and will soon publish a website dedicated to my writing, which I hope will help others to believe that they too can make the journey to overjoyed from overwhelmed.

Much love, Wendy

19th March 2018

Dear Jenny

For the first time I am writing to you from home. As I have continued on this journey, moving steadily in the direction of being 'me', I find I have been writing more poetry at home and I now feel that I can also find the peace I need to write to you as I look over the fields and hills of home. This is another huge step forward for me Jenny. I am also telling many more people about my writing and feeling confident enough to mention my book when I present to large business groups. Many people say they will buy it, so that is very encouraging!

My youngest daughter has just flown out to India to meet my son and wife, who have been travelling in Nepal, India and Sri Lanka for the past seven months and so I have three weeks now where things are a little more peaceful and definitely tidier! When I look back over the past two years, I feel so incredibly lucky that I discovered the peace of the monastery, your wisdom and kindness, my new practices and more recently new associates to work with whose beliefs align with mine. I cannot believe how much my priorities have changed.

Work is not the 'be all and end all' of my days. I can read my body and know immediately if I am overtired or becoming stressed. I know how to cure this and I walk the walk. My relationship with all my children is stronger than ever and my relationship with my mother is finally in a far better place. I have learned so much about how we are programmed and how our thoughts shape our worlds.

I have been enabled to keep true to the values of my work, supporting business owners, but in changing the shape of my business from that of an employer with offices and training rooms, to that of a consultant working from home with wonderful associates, I have brought flexibility and space to each working day and week.

I know that I am at a point in life where my children are grown and my Mum is now being cared for and so these transitions have possibly been easier for me than a younger parent, but many of the changes I have made involve only minutes a day or a change of priority or thought. It is not easy to change the habits of a lifetime and I have sometimes lost my way a little as you know, but something deep inside kept me going and the journey has been so worthwhile.

I start my days with a gentle wake up and affirmation routine, I use Heartmath throughout the day and I end my day by writing my journal and then saying thank you to every part of my body and sending my love to family and friends. I cannot believe how much appreciating the little things makes me smile and how much happier I feel because I am smiling. I sing in the car again, I dance around the kitchen again, I sit in a café on a Saturday and cannot believe how lucky I am.

I stand and listen to birdsong, I laugh when I'm walking and the wind is nearly blowing me over and I rejoice in nature every day. Probably the most amazing thing is that I can now empty my mind, something I never believed was possible. Not for hours, that will take years more practice, but for good stretches, especially when I am walking the hills and moors or sitting in the temple of Samye Ling.

I am increasingly sharing the lessons I have learned with clients and over the past nine months, have spent many hours listening to busy professionals, who may be business owners or are leading teams in education or the public sector. They are exhausted, stressed, unfulfilled, miserable. I coached someone the other day who literally had cried all weekend and they didn't know why. I persuaded her to down tools and find some space for four days – she says I possibly saved her life. Stopping everything and going to a peaceful and beautiful place made her think about 'Why'. I suggested that whilst she was away she asked herself the following:

Why am I working myself into the ground?
Why am I setting such punishing deadlines?
Why am I not sleeping?
Why am I so anxious all the time?
Why am I not me anymore?

191

These as you know Jenny, are the very same questions I was asking myself two years ago.

Because so many people I coach are struggling with these questions, I have designed a six day retreat on the Isle of Mull. I'm running it for the first time this April and am including some of the learning I have been lucky enough to receive as I have travelled this incredible journey. Leadership Embodiment, Heartmath, walking, time to read and reflect and trusting your inner voice are all elements of the programme. I am hopeful that the ten women attending will find the courage to change their lives as I have done and as you did too, all those years ago.

I intend to run regular retreats in the future because I have personally discovered that it is only when you truly stop and get off the hamster wheel you have created, that you can step away from the role you believe the world wants you to play and consider the gifts you were born with. These are your truth and yours to give to the world.

However, I also believe every one of us can make small shifts in our every day. We can find five minutes to breathe correctly and look at the dew on a leaf. We can pause and really listen to another, we can find the courage to be ourselves in every conversation we have. We can allow ourselves to put ourselves first. It is not selfish to love oneself. Buddha says "You can search throughout the entire universe for someone who is more deserving of your love and affection than you are yourself, and that person is not to be found anywhere. You yourself, as much as anybody in the entire universe deserve your love and affection."

Jenny, I am sure you will agree that in these fast-moving times, more and more people in the West are heading towards burn out. We are racing through life at a terrifying speed, eating and drinking on the go, scared of missing a single email in case we are 'seen' as not being serious about work. Young women are filled with guilt as they are torn between motherhood and careers they have invested ten plus years in. Older women are sandwiched between caring for teenagers and parents as they try to supplement family incomes. I sincerely hope that the increasing focus on the role and treatment of women will force change.

We also hear daily about the effects of living with continuous stress; from millions of working days costing the economy billions, to the heart-breaking individual stories of chronic and terminal illness. Surely these findings will start to have some impact on the way we currently work? In the meantime, individuals have to find ways to bring some 'slow' into every day. I know I have managed to do this by embedding heart-focused breathing into my every day and changing the way I work. What I am trying to do as I coach and write is share my learning, which is why I have decided to publish these letters in a book and include the walks that have inspired me and the poetry I have written and perform. I hope that in doing so the letters find their way to you and you will understand how profound an influence you have been in my life.

I do not know you Jenny, I only met you for a total of about two hours, but you changed me forever. I will never be able to thank you enough.

With my love and sincere thanks

Wendy

Postscript

It is some fifteen months since I wrote my final letter to Jenny and I feel, dear Reader, that I should bring you up to date, for a lot happens in a year. I am still visiting Samye Ling, finding comfort in the calm of the monastery and inspiration in the surrounding fells. My interest in Leadership Embodiment has deepened, I attended a further course and met two wonderful trainers; they introduced the practice to women who attended our retreats in the Yorkshire Dales and in Scotland. It is heartening to see the learning I have embraced over the past three years, work its magic on other tired souls.

I read daily, learning from wise teachers such as Wayne Dyer and Greg Braden. I love the rejuvinating works of Parker J Palmer, whom I was introduced to via the content on the pen-drive given to me by that wise, kind monk on my first visit to Samye Ling. Parker is the founder of the Center for Courage and Renewal, based in Seattle, Washington State, USA. What began in 1993 as a quiet experiment in sustaining the inner life of public educators has grown into an educational non-profit, fostering courage and renewal across all professions. His work is recognised globally as a force for change and the teachings he has developed cultivate the heart and soul. I was privileged to attend one of his courses in Wales last Autumn and found the experience deeply moving. If you have not come across his work, please do take a look – his writings are beautiful and powerful and his teachings are much needed in this crazy world we are creating.

I try to walk every day and write about many of my longer walks, jotting down notes as I walk and then publishing the walks on my website, so that others may enjoy them. Walking gives me space, away from work and responsibilities, to rest my mind; and often nature brings me the gift of poetry or ideas for new ways to help others. I share much of my poetry on my website and increasingly use it in my work. Inviting leaders to contemplate and discuss a poem is a great way to encourage open conversations and allow individuals to explore feelings.

In the early part of this past year, the content of my book started to take shape and the Universe sent me generous people to read and edit the letters. I arranged an evening of poetry and readings at our local bookshop, with good feedback and so, six months ago, I was ready to pull together the different sections of the book and excited about its release.

But then, in the same week, my first grand-child was born and my Mum passed away and so my world was turned upside down.

Most of us have experienced the death of a loved one by the time we are in middle age and we must all grieve in our own way. We have to deal with the rawness of grief as we move on through life; eating, working, looking after family. For me, losing my remaining parent pulled the rug from under me. Instead of the relief I thought I would feel seeing my Mum freed from her suffering, all I felt was a loss of my own identity. Who was I, if I was no longer a daughter? Who really knew me now?

My Mum was not the easiest of women, but she gave me the gift of this precious life and now she was gone. I felt like all my strength had been 'zapped'. I delivered client's work and presented at events I had committed to, fastening my smile in place as I entered a room. But inside, I felt lost and closed down. My morning routine, my breathing techniques, my centering affirmations all felt too much like hard work and all but disappeared, as grief rolled over me.

Preferring my own company to that of others, I continued to walk and this was my salvation. Eventually, as trees blossomed and curlews returned to the moor, I started to feel connected to the world again.

I spoke to a trusted and wise colleague, who gently reminded me that I needed space. Just as I had three years ago when, ill and broken, I was taken to Samye Ling. I needed time to let myself heal. Not just the few days I had taken off work the week Mum died, but real space. However, accepting the fact that I was entitled to 'just be' was very hard for me, even after all my learning.

Once I'd made the decision to allow myself time, I felt a huge sense of relief. I re-committed to my daily practices of Leadership Embodiment and Heartmath, writing my journal and giving thanks for all my blessings. Physically, this practice increases the feel good hormones in the body, mentally, it takes the brain out of fight and flight mode which enables clear thinking, spiritually, it sooths one's soul.

I know I am lucky to be able to make this choice, many people must return to work after compassionate leave and somehow keep going. I hope they find comfort from friends and support groups and give themselves time to find their own ways of healing.

So, here I am, writing the last few lines of Words, Walks, Wisdom. Every day, things remind me of Mum, but I know she would not want me to be sad. My new grand-daughter is a joy and a constant reminder that life goes on. I am the bridge between all the generations past and all those to come, as we all are.

We may have many lives, in many different forms, but we are only aware of this one and so I entreat you, live it well. Slow down, breathe deeply and appreciate the moments. Give yourself time, my friend. Love with all your heart, enjoy your friendships, hold your children close, choose kindness and most importantly of all, love the person in the mirror.

I hope this book encourages you to bring some space into your every day, and that you are enjoying the incredible gift of life. If you would like to learn more about how you too can make some positive changes, please follow this link to download a free 20 minute lesson.

https://www.wendybowers.co.uk/wisdom

And with that, I will leave you with a final poem and my heartfelt wishes that you too, can 'uncover the key'.

The Key

We build our own prisons and fashion the bars
With the metal of money, mortgage and cars.
Blinkered, we chase the material dream
Because 'things' are the way to prove we are seen.
The more we amass, the less we achieve
The more we control, the less we believe
The faster we run, the less we can see
The prison gate's locked and we can't find the key.

We're running so fast we can only look down
We haven't got time to look up or look round,
We're piling on pressure, we're taking the meds
We're asleep in the day and awake in our beds
We're killing creative, we're murdering soul
We're losing our insight, we're scoring own goals
And where are we running and what's the reward
Another 10 laps of our own prison yard?

Stop fucking running! Slow it right down,
Lift up your head from the path you have ground.
Take off the blinkers, look at the sky
Doesn't its beauty make you want to cry?
Unplug the TV, switch off the screen
Stand in a field and hear yourself scream
Ask yourself 'why' again and again
Ask yourself 'who' and 'what for' and 'what then'
Then shut up and listen and sink to your knees
As the voice from within uncovers the key.

Acknowledgements:

My warmest thanks to the following people, who helped me in so many ways, to bring my first book to fruition.

Firstly to all at Kagyu Samye Ling in Eskdalemuir. Your welcome, understanding and care were key to my recovery from illness and the peace I found in your temple and grounds, enabled me to find my writing again.

I am particularly grateful to Laura Ridings – who gave many hours of her own time to firstly, help me build and maintain my website and secondly, undertake the massive task of the book layout. Her generosity and patience will be hard to repay. Thank you Laura, you are a very special lady.

Special thanks also to Terry Marsh – a hugely successful author of travel and writing guides, who was kind enough to personally answer an email I sent to his publisher commenting on a walk in his book, 'Great Mountain Days in the Pennines.' He then continued our correspondence, gave me oodles of helpful advice and also edited the letters section of the book, simply from the goodness of his heart. This world needs more people like Terry who, although they are already busy enough, find time to offer support and guidance to new writers. Terry, there's a copy of my book on its way to you with love and thanks.

To my wonderful friends and mentors who encouraged me to keep writing, thank you – you know who you are. To those who offered to be my 'readers' diligently poring over the book in draft form, checking for errors and offering valuable feedback, thank you Elaine, Helen and Tracy.

There are sadly, some people no longer with us, who deserve my heartfelt thanks.
These special people ignited something in me that compelled me to write and for many years, shared their love of poetry, drama and reading with me. These are my parents of course, Greta Wilkinson (my elocution and drama teacher) and my favourite primary school teacher Mr Dan Packer, who encouraged all his pupils to write a weekly diary. To this day, I still write my journal almost daily.

My children, Laura, Amy, David and Katie, are wiser than myself by far. They are resilient, bold, intelligent, hardworking, talented, fun and kind. I am immensely proud of them all.

And finally, my love and deepest thanks to Glenn, who has always sacrificed his dreams so that I could follow mine.

Printed in Poland
by Amazon Fulfillment
Poland Sp. z o.o., Wrocław